To Mary,

Enjoy this book and I wish you the best in your future. Remember you are capable of anything and everything that you desire!

Be well!

Dr Young :)

The 3 STEP PROCESS for
Transforming your Mindset
Overcoming your Fears and
Harnessing Unimaginable Success

FOUNDATION
FOCUS
FREEDOM

TERENCE YOUNG, M.D.

Foundation Focus Freedom

Copyright © 2018 by Terence Young, MD
All rights reserved. No part of this book may be reproduced or transmitted in any form or by any means, electronic or mechanical, including photocopying, recording, or by any information storage and retrieval system without the written permission of the author, except where permitted by law.

The "Pomodoro Technique®" and "Pomodoro®" are registered trademarks by Francesco Cirillo.

ISBN: 978-1-7328535-2-2
Young Phoenix Enterprises, LLC
www.terenceyoungmd.com
www.docdeliversbooks.com
Danville, IL

TABLE OF CONTENTS

SECTION 1

INTRODUCTION 1

CHAPTER 1 3
WHO AM I? 3
CHAPTER 2 13
THE OVERALL CONCEPT OF THE SYSTEM 13

SECTION 2

LEVEL 1: FOUNDATION 19

CHAPTER 3 21
BUILDING YOUR FOUNDATION 21
CHAPTER 4 25
UNDERSTANDING YOUR LIMITING BELIEFS
AND DEVELOPING YOUR "WHY" 25
CHAPTER 5 35
DISCOVERING YOUR "WHY" 35

SECTION 3

LEVEL 2: FOCUS 41

CHAPTER 6 43
UNDERSTANDING YOUR "CIRCLE OF CONCEPTION" 43
CHAPTER 7 47
YOUR FIRST TRIMESTER: BE 47
   Developing Your Core *48*
   Identifying Your Focus *52*
   Reinforcing Your "BE" and Establishing Your "STATE" *55*
CHAPTER 8 79
YOUR SECOND TRIMESTER: DO 79
CHAPTER 9 87
F.E.A.R. (AND THE THINGS YOU DO TO GET PAST IT) 87
   Enhancing Your Language to Overcome Fear *108*

    Enhancing Your Physical Reaction to Fear............................ 120
    Taking the R.I.G.H.T. Action 139
    Reengage... 156
CHAPTER 10 159
YOUR THIRD TRIMESTER: SEE 159
    Building Block 1: Seeing a Familiar Scenario 182
    Building Block 2: Adding Emotions to
    Your Visual Picture and Enhancing the Scene 186
    Building Block 3: Seeing Yourself
    Express Your Core Values 190
    Building Block 4: Seeing Yourself
    Achieve Your Outcome.. 196
CHAPTER 11 203
YOUR DELIVERY: REBIRTH AND LEARNING HOW TO "ACT" 203
    Asking the Right Questions 211
    Overview of Your 90-Day Outcome Plan System 225

SECTION 4

LEVEL 3: FREEDOM **243**

CHAPTER 12 245
    What is F.R.E.E.D.O.M.?... 246
    How Does This Relate to HAVE? 251
CHAPTER 13 265
IN CLOSING….. 265
CHAPTER 14 267
BONUS SESSION 267
ACKNOWLEDGEMENTS.. 269

SECTION 1
INTRODUCTION

Chapter 1
Who am I?

My name is Dr. Terence Young and I have had the privilege and the pleasure of being able to serve people as a physician in the field of obstetrics and gynecology for over 22 years.

My outcome is to present you with a system that has been transformational in my life. Not just my life, but in the lives of those that I have taught it to as well. And once you learn it, you will learn how to live a more fulfilled life, with passion and purpose. You will start to feel that you are not just living day to day, but you are alive and thriving every day.

During my transition from being a full-time doctor to full-time entrepreneur, I've encountered many victories and losses. The wins put me in a state of excitement and euphoria and the lows brought me down to levels of sadness and frustration that almost made me want to quit my journey—my transformation towards becoming an enhanced version of myself.

Now, you may wonder why a physician of 22 years decided to step away from what was comfortable, financially secure and "safe" to enter the realm of entrepreneurship. Well, the reason is simpler than you think, and many people can relate to it.

My life was frustrating me many years ago because I was living someone else's. Like many others, I was frustrated, overwhelmed and unfulfilled because I wasn't walking my own path to get to the life that I desired. I was walking someone else's path to get the life that they desired.

Jim Rohn described it best with this powerful quote:

"If you don't design your own life plan, chances are you'll fall into someone else's plan. And guess what they have planned for you? Not much."

So, the purpose of this book is to provide you with a simple system and pathway that will support and guide you, as it has me and those that I have worked with. I will help you to overcome your fears and challenges in life, conceive your dreams and deliver an enhanced version of you.

You will develop the proper mindset to focus on your success.

You will identify, address, and overcome the fears that are holding you back from taking the necessary action that moves your life forward.

You will be empowered with the freedom of designing the goals and outcomes that will be transformative.

But before we do that, I would like to take the next 60 seconds to describe to you how to get the most out of reading this book. It's a very simple four step process that will help you develop the proper mindset to maximize your results.

The first step is that you took the time to invest in yourself and get this book. Congratulations to you for being ahead of the curve!

The second step is to find out exactly where you are in life and what you are looking for. This step is about being honest and open with yourself about where you are in life and where you want to be. You will move forward faster towards what you desire when you have a clear and honest understanding of where you are now. This is the time to get real with yourself, not hold back from playing full-out, and answer the tough questions which you may have avoided in the past.

Step three is about learning the abundance of techniques and strategies I will lay out for you. Think of these strategies and techniques like that old-school black bag that physicians used to carry around. They would have so many tools and items that could treat a variety of different ailments and each one had its purpose. Here, I'm going to present you with multiple tools and items in the form of assignments. Some are verbal, some mental, and others are physical in the form of written documentation.

The fourth step is about putting the techniques and strategies that resonate with you into action, becoming that new and enhanced YOU! Those will be the ones that will empower you the most, getting you quicker to the outcomes that you desire. It will be as simple as mastering two or three tools in order to get the best out of you!

You may ask, what is my reasoning for wanting to help other people achieve their dreams?

As far back as I can remember, I have had this burning desire to help others. I knew this was what I was put on this earth to do. With my youthful energy and can-do attitude, no one could stop me.

There was a moment in high school when I had a meeting with my counselor, feeling excited about telling her my chosen path in life and then, it turned all to crap. I remember storming out of the guidance counselor's office after the meeting.

Why?

I was pissed!

After confidently stating that my goal in life was to become a doctor, she curtly and plainly informed me that I should aim lower.

Aim lower?!

As much as it stung that she didn't believe in me, I didn't let that stop me. I followed my dream to go to college even though my guidance counselor said I wasn't going to make it. Medical school was hard. Despite this, many of the doctors told me that I was one of the hardest working and best students they'd ever seen.

But exams were a constant struggle and the anxiety sometimes got to me. After failing the same exam twice, I was threatened to be expelled if I failed another one. The school even forced me to take an IQ test and go to meditation classes to prove that I belonged. It was almost like being in that counselor's office again, only this time all my hard work and years of my life were on the line.

On my third try, I passed the exam with flying colors.

I vowed to never fail a test again. And I never did.

I completed my residency at Emory University, one of top ten residency programs in the country. And after four grueling years of 90-hour workweeks, I graduated with one of the highest starting salaries.

I was beaming with joy! I had arrived.

For the next 15 years, I lived my childhood dream—delivering babies, performing complex surgeries, and serving in women's health care. The hours were long, and the work was tiring, but this had been what I had put all my heart and soul into.

Then, in the fall of 2011, something much unexpected happened…

It was any another work day. I just finished up a routine patient visit when I was called into the Department Director's office.

"Terence, you haven't made the income we expected. We are going to let you go."

My stomach dropped.

Fired!?!

This cannot be happening to me.

Dazed, I sat staring into the distance, my mind fixated on the diamond ring I had just bought my fiancée and the image of the life we had envisioned for our family. Completely devastated, I had no idea what I'd do next.

I took a good look inside. I loved my career as a physician, but I could feel myself getting burned out by the business side of it all. I had set out to help people on a massive scale. It was my purpose to make a difference… not be just another faceless employee in the corporate machine. It was time to take my life's work to the next level and help others on an even larger scale. It was time to take on my biggest and most difficult fear—going into business for myself.

It took more than just the verbal decision. I like to say, "Instead of delivering babies I delivered a NEW ME." I created a shift in my mindset and habits.

And it changed EVERYTHING.

Now, I am making an impact on people's lives by showing them how to experience the same freedom I have. No more 90-hour workweeks or missed date nights. I will never forget the feeling in my stomach the moment I saw my wife's face when I had to cancel yet ANOTHER date night between us because I was mentally and physically exhausted.

This job that I worked so many hours and spent so much time studying to achieve was sucking the life out of the things that were most important. Life was happening, and I was just plodding away on the corporate hamster wheel.

Fast forward six years later…

I am providing my wife with the quality of life she deserved and was promised to her the moment she walked down the aisle. And now we have more date nights than ever. We are laughing about things that would normally have been huge stressors, all because I was able to…

Cut down hours, make my own schedule, and build my own business.

These were things that were only a glimmer of a dream six years before. Now, I get to focus on what is truly important in life while bettering people's lives—emotionally, spiritually, and financially.

I've been where you are at. Feeling overwhelmed at home and work with the responsibilities and challenges. Being scared and worried that I would never live the life that I desired. One with passion, excited about what I do each day, feeling happy and complete.

The truth is that if I can do it, so can you! As someone that lives a life serving and helping others, I will be your guide to help you overcome your fears, challenges, and obstacles in life. As I transition away from the corporate world, I have more time to guide others towards what they desire in their own lives. It's fulfilling for me to know that I can help so many people live a happier life.

When I started my journey, I was just like you; I wanted to have the freedom to live life on my own terms. I began studying the habits and actions of successful people to learn their secrets to achieving all the things in life they desired. I found the one thing that they had in common was their mindset.

People that strive for achieving freedom in their life often hit a critical crossroads. They are either the type of person who knows what they want in life, starts on their intended pathway, but gets derailed because of fear and loss of focus. Or, they are the type of person who doesn't know exactly what they desire in life, but they know they want to achieve more. However, fear or lack of focus prevents them from even starting on the pathway.

Either the onset of fear or the lack of focus will prevent people from achieving the freedom that they desire in their lives. This freedom can come in many different forms depending on the pathway that someone chooses in their life. So how does freedom look to you?

We are going to review questions that may cause uncomfortable feelings to arise within. Notice them because they will help you push out of your comfort zone to the next level.

Are you seeking freedom from a job or a career path that you feel does not serve you?

Are you looking for freedom to be able to express yourself more optimally in a relationship?

Do you seek the freedom to be in a relationship and be the person that you truly are and not the person that your partner desires you to be?

Are you seeking the freedom to live by a means financially when you have less stress and worry about your own financial situation?

Are you seeking the freedom to escape your current level of physical health and live a more optimal and healthier lifestyle?

If you are, then wonderful because you can achieve what you desire. Just a small shift with your thinking, combined with the proper actions, will help you move towards the life that you desire.

Thus, I created this book for you! As I stated in the beginning, mindset is the common denominator that is the key to optimizing your life's path towards the freedom that you desire.

Mindset is simply two components, your actions and thoughts that you are aware of, and the actions and thoughts that you are unaware of. The former being your conscious mind and the latter being your unconscious mind. I will guide you along your journey, helping you to enhance your mindset, consciously and unconsciously. By doing this, your journey towards the freedom that you desire will become easier and more fun for you. Communication with yourself is the key to getting unstuck from the life that you have and truly living the life that you desire.

Let's just be honest and have a real conversation with one another.

Are you up for that?

Most of us know what it takes to be successful in life or to achieve the things or outcomes that we desire. For example, we know that the key to having a healthier lifestyle involves proper diet and exercise.

We understand that to have a more effective and harmonious relationship with our partners, communication is the key.

Finally, we understand that to have more success financially, we need to effectively execute the steps in our lives that are more productive and eliminate the steps that are not as productive.

Despite this, we still work the jobs in our lives that we are not happy with, feeling like a useless cog in the machine, wasting our creativity and free thought away, having no motivation and losing passion along the way.

Thus, we know how to do the things that will get us the life that we desire, however, we may not clearly see the path between what we desire and achieving that outcome. The good news is that there are two essential things to achieve what you desire. The more successful people do this very effectively, incorporating the components, often at times without realizing they are doing so.

So, what are these two components, you ask?

They are:

1. Visualization of their future success

2. Taking action despite fear

So why are these two components so important? There is an established concept, which you may have heard in the past that is described as, "Be, Do and Have." Simply, you ask yourself, "Who do I need to **be**, what are the things that I need to **do** and what will I **have** after I achieved it?" People who are more successful take this to the next level by incorporating visualization and taking action despite fear.

I model successful people and incorporate the two components that I previously mentioned, visualizing, and taking action. In the traditional "Be, Do and Have," we ask ourselves the simple question:

"Who is the person that we have to **BE** in order to **DO** the things that we desire so that we can **HAVE** the life that we want?"

For example, the optimal way to utilize this powerful perspective is to have a mindset such as this:

"By being happy with positive thoughts, I will do the things in my life that are more productive and efficient and then I will have more success with my desired outcomes."

Now unfortunately, most people alter the order and wonder why they are not able to achieve the things that they desire in life. It's because they have the total concept backwards. Thinking and living with a mindset such as this:

"When I **have** more money in life, I will be able to **do** the things that I desire and thus, I will **be** happier."

Did you notice how the order is backwards?

In the latter sentence, one is operating from the mindset of have, do and be.

This is completely backwards and it's the reason why, many people will continue to struggle to achieve the things that they desire in life. However, when you have the order correctly as be, do and have, you are setting yourself up with the proper foundation, as I stated in the beginning.

You are setting yourself up with the correct ***mindset*** for success.

However, I felt that this definition was incomplete. After studying and observing successful people, I realized that it didn't emphasize two critical components which are essential for optimizing the process.

These two missing components—visualization and action, enhance this, allowing you to increase your efforts towards what you desire.

So, instead of the traditional definition:

We now define it as:

When I think of DO in the original concept, it's more about having the mindset or internal thoughts of knowing something has to be done, which is important.

However, translating what you need to "DO" into its physical component requires the process of taking ACTION. Once I separated out this key component from the DO, I began to realize that ACTION is the key to physically manifesting the things that you want.

Just as important, visualizing your success as if it has already occurred, will be a powerful tool in your arsenal during your journey. The order is critical in the equation because it is essential to SEE yourself (by using visualization) as the person that you wish to become THEN you ACT to make your internal visualizations a physical manifestation. This is how I transformed my life and so shall you!

Chapter 2
The Overall Concept of the System

The concept of be, do and have will be expanded upon, incorporating the two essentials of visualization and taking action.

Before I guide you towards the things that you desire externally, you must first work on your internal being. Imagine the process as a kind of rebirth.

You start by rewiring your internal being because the mindset that you have now is not working for you. If you don't have the correct internal mindset you are not going to be able to achieve the things externally that you desire.

So, you must breakdown the parts of your internal thought process so that you can be better equipped to help you achieve the things externally in the world that you desire. Once you can do this, it will make it much easier for you to plan for and achieve the things that you desire in your own life. As you enhance your internal and external thoughts, you will experience a wonderful transformation. Knowing who you wish to *be*, *doing* the things that you love, *visualizing* your success now, taking the *action* you need, finally *having* the outcomes that you desire.

Level one is your foundation. Think of it like a couple who wants to have optimal health before pregnancy.

Just like when welcoming a new baby boy or girl into your family, steps must be taken before you start your journey to ensure you are developing the right environment for a healthy and successful rebirth of the new you! Here, I will define what limiting beliefs are and how to overcome them. I will also identify what core values are and how to define your own.

Level two is your focus. You will discover the person who you wish to BE and learn what you need to DO *internally* in order to overcome your fears. Next, you will learn about the first of the two critical components of successful people and SEE your success now. You will learn how to ACT *externally* and push past your fears, the second critical component of successful people. Finally, you will begin to see how to HAVE and keep what you have achieved.

As you transform your life within level two, your growth occurs in stages, like the trimesters of pregnancy. Each trimester develops you more, preparing for your actual transformation.

Level three is your freedom. You have presented yourself to the world, transformed into the person and life that you desire! Here is where the real growth and development occurs. You have the basic tools for survival, but a helping hand will keep you safe and nourished as you continue to enhance yourself.

You will understand what freedom truly is.

As you transition through Foundation, Focus, and Freedom, your internal growth and development will allow the external manifestations of what you desire to become clearer, more focused, and easier to accomplish.

The biggest obstacle to achieving success and manifesting your desires is not any external manifestations but the internal thoughts and limiting beliefs that you create for yourself.

Asking yourself the right questions and rewiring your internal mindset builds the foundation that your new successful life needs. It will allow you to follow through with your goals and achieve outcomes more effectively. Which in turn gives you the freedom to grow into an even more enhanced version of yourself.

Have you ever played darts or maybe watched a match?

Not many people can consistently hit the bullseye but it's possible with a lot of practice and effort. This is why hitting the bullseye gives you the maximum value of points, rewarding those who have the precision and skills to hit the center.

Your internal being is that bullseye. That target that can be challenging to develop but when it has been explored, nurtured and enhanced, it will provide your life with rewards and manifestations that you can't even imagine.

Some people are simply happy to just hit the damn dartboard, but you are not that person. You wouldn't be or else you wouldn't have picked up this book and taken the first steps towards your internal and external transformation!

Imagine a dartboard with a bullseye and two outer rings. They represent the three main concepts of our overall platform.

Your life is like this dartboard, with your internal self represented by the core or bullseye of who you are, and your external self represented by the two outer rings.

The core or bullseye is your foundation.

The middle ring is your focus.

The outer ring is your freedom.

We are going to learn how to hit all three targets. I'm excited to present this to you because my outcome is to help you conceive your dreams, overcome your fears and challenges, and deliver a transformed you!

I have seen how this approach has helped my own life, and those around me who I have shared the process with, and now I get to share it with you as well!

Pay attention because this part is very important!

I want you to congratulate yourself for taking the time to invest in yourself because you are worth it.

Unlike most people in this world, you decided today to take action by getting this book and reading the introduction. Many people get books, bring them home and say they are going to start it "later" but later never comes. I must admit, I've done it before and I have the unread books on my shelves to prove it!

However, you are different because you took action and that needs to be rewarded, so take the time to congratulate yourself because you will begin to realize that this is a turning point in your life.

Today, you have made the commitment to yourself that you will use your focus and energy to strive towards delivering an enhanced version of yourself. Most people don't have that level of strength or courage like you do.

Would you agree that it's important to have a better understanding of yourself, where you are right now in life?

Is it safe to say that there are areas of your life that can be improved upon or enhanced, like your family relationships, financial situations or health?

Do you believe that with even a *little effort* each day, you will move closer towards the person that you desire?

Then believing this, you will see the importance of taking the time each day to read just a few pages of the book, absorbing the content and doing the work that is required and necessary to get the most. And I'm not talking about getting the most out of the book. More importantly, I'm talking about getting the most out of you, unlocking your inner potential that is just itching to be released!

Realize that you are an amazing person, worthy of everything and anything that you desire, but the sad thing is most people don't believe or even realize this. What I have seen, time and time again, is this:

Many people in your life, even though they mean well and think they know better than you, will share the same message. They may be your family, friends, those closest to you who have the most sway and influence upon you. There will even be people who come out of nowhere, just to tell you…

YOU CAN'T DO IT

They are the ones who gave up or failed to achieve the dreams that they had or even worse, let fear hold them back from even starting in the first place. For the most part, they mean well (some might just be straight up mean), wanting to subtly suggest that what you are attempting to do is not feasible or doable. They are blinded by their own setbacks and failures, not wanting you to succeed.

Some do this because they really care about you and want you to avoid the pain of failure, because they have been there. Others are just acting selfishly, consciously or unconsciously, because your success means they get to be in their own failure alone, without having someone else to help justify their own lack of success.

Are you familiar with the **crab in the barrel** mentality?

If you love eating crabs like I used to (well, I'm vegan now and still miss them), you may have seen a barrel of crabs, freshly pulled from the Carolina coast, alive and thriving. Have you ever seen a top on the barrel to keep the crabs from escaping?

I've never seen it.

Why is that? Because they can't escape the barrel.

There is always one at the top, ready to get out and I route for that little blue crab to reach his freedom but at the last minute, one or two claws grab that poor crab and pull him back down. Never to escape and destined to live a life of being committed to the dinner plate.

That's family. Friends. Loved ones.

Pulling you back into the barrel of failure, destined to lead a life of unfilled dreams or even worse, being comfortable, not striving for anything more. They pull you back because they are in the middle or near the top of their own barrels of life. They may see a little sliver of light but can't reach it because someone or something holds them back.

And now they do it to you!

The reality is they are not committed to their dreams like you are. They had a choice to move forward, despite the challenges and obstacles but chose to quit.

Not you!

You, on the other hand, had the courage to make the choice to rise up, commit to overcoming your fears and challenges, and start fulfilling your dreams to deliver an enhanced version of yourself!

Don't fall into the trap of incorporating their fears. They are not yours, they are theirs. Don't let them tell you that you can't do it because you absolutely freaking can!

They may tell you that you can't do it, but understand this:

You can't quit because you are their hope for escaping the barrel of their unfilled dreams. They need you to escape, give birth to that enhanced version of yourself and help pull them out of their own barrel. When the day is done, and you have finished this book and moved forward in your life in unimaginable ways, realize that your job is not done. It's your time to reach down and help the next person out.

And here is the beautiful thing that I have seen in myself and those who understand the process, and you will see yourself in time as you progress through your own growth. They will relax their grip on fears, released from their own doubts, and ask you, "How did you do it?" People who once were critical of you and shared their negative energy will have a polar shift and begin to seek your support and guidance. It's a beautiful thing to watch!

So, can you make the commitment today that you will shake loose those claws around you, move forward despite the obstacles, challenges and setbacks and keep moving forward towards the person that you will be reborn into? Yes, or yes?

Wonderful! I'm glad to hear that!

Remember, you are an unstoppable force, so don't let anyone get in the way of delivering the enhanced version of you because in the famous words of Napoleon Hill:

"Whatever the mind of man can conceive and believe, it can achieve."

SECTION 2
Level 1: Foundation

Chapter 3
Building Your Foundation

One of the best parts of my time in corporate health care, outside of delivering cute little babies, was when I got to meet the future parent or parents before there even was a pregnancy. This time is known as the **preconception care**. This is the magical time when parents start getting prepared for their upcoming pregnancy. They want to do everything they can to ensure an optimal and healthy one.

They typically will come in with list upon list of questions asking about what they should eat and how they should exercise. What they should and shouldn't do and when they should or shouldn't do it. The point being that great care and thought go into the birth of an infant and just as much care and preparation should go into your own development as well.

I remember one young couple that went so far as to come to the office, check off all the boxes of the questions that they had and then wanted feedback on their birthing plan. Now this plan was really detailed. The couple was very specific regarding how often they were monitored in labor, who would be present, and many other requests.

Now you may think its extreme for someone to go through a detailed plan, but this is the exact mindset that you need to have as you start your journey towards becoming an enhanced version of yourself. If you were that couple that was anticipating growing their family, bringing new life into the world, wouldn't you want to take that same care and preparation in order to optimize your chances for success?

We're essentially doing the same thing because as we go through this process of **preconception care**, followed by the **Circle of Conception**, and concluded with your **post conception care**, we are stacking the stages one by one from your preconceptual care to the newly delivered you. Or more simply in your case, from the person that you are right now into the person that you wish to become in the future.

During this preconception care, there are two tools that you will learn about. They are limiting beliefs and developing your "why."

Think of these tools like prenatal vitamins.

Would a woman be able to conceive, go through pregnancy, and have a successful delivery without taking a single prenatal vitamin? Absolutely, it can be done. However, is this the healthiest pathway? Something as small as a prenatal vitamin provides an immense amount of nutritional support that is essential for the optimal growth and development of the newborn child, and who wouldn't want their baby to be the healthiest it could be?

As you start the process of building your foundation, I challenge you to be open minded to the concepts that are being presented. You may decide that:

You already know the answers to the questions that I'm presenting.

That it may seem childish and immature and it doesn't make much sense.

You want to just get to the good stuff and have me tell you how to create goals and outcomes and be successful at doing so.

The way that you will get the most out of this book is by not taking the little things for granted. I challenge you to complete all the exercises that are presented in the book because what may seem small and insignificant to you, like a prenatal vitamin, is more powerful than you can ever realize!

So, are you ready to start taking your first vitamins?

Excellent!

It's essential for both men and women to take vitamins in life, optimizing their health and well-being. Thus, the two vitamins that you will take are:

    1. Understanding and busting limiting beliefs

2. Developing your "why"

So, here's your first pill. Grab a glass of water, get yourself hydrated, and let's swallow up some nutrition to help optimize your mindset for this journey.

Chapter 4
Understanding Your Limiting Beliefs and Developing Your "Why"

So, what are limiting beliefs? They are the thoughts, consciously or unconsciously, that you have about a situation. They are limiting because these beliefs that hold you back from achieving the things that you desire in your life. And because you have trained your mind to believe that they are your reality, you are crippled from moving forward in productive ways. For example, a limiting belief may be "I don't have the time to exercise" or "I don't have the money to start the career that I desire."

The purpose for understanding limiting beliefs is that they are your internal voice that says you can't become the person that you desire, do the things that you wish to in life, or manifest the things you want.

Let's identify the limiting beliefs that are holding you back from achieving your ultimate dreams and squash them!

By defining, then redefining and in time, eliminating your limiting beliefs, you are nurturing your mindset in the early stages of your growth development. By the time you get to achieving the outcomes that you desire not only will they be successful, you may be pleasantly surprised to see that you have far exceeded your own expectations.

"You will never achieve it if you don't believe it." – Terence Young, MD

This was perhaps said best by Napoleon Hill in his book, "Think and Grow Rich."

"Whatever the mind can conceive and believe, it can achieve." – Napoleon Hill

Types of limiting beliefs

There are three major areas where self-limiting beliefs reside. For many of us, we have been raised with these beliefs and accept them as normal:

Personal limiting beliefs

Social limiting beliefs

Financial limiting beliefs

When you have a **personal limiting belief,** these would include things regarding your beliefs around time or self-confidence. Regarding time, you may believe that you don't have enough time in the day to take on a new project. You may believe that since you didn't achieve what you desired in the past, you have missed your window of opportunity to do it today. Limiting beliefs around time can also represent not believing that you have time in the future or that your window of time in the past has come and gone. Self-confidence limiting beliefs would include the belief that only smart people are successful or that you are too old to learn a new skill in life.

Social limiting beliefs arise from what you believe others will think or say about you. For example, you may believe that if you don't succeed, you will be criticized by others. Or you may believe that since you have had failure in the past, it will inevitably happen again with something new and you will be mocked and ridiculed.

Finally, **financial limiting beliefs** revolve around your feelings regarding money. Believing that working hard is the only way to make money is a self-limiting belief. Believing that higher education is the only way to get the best jobs would be a self-limiting belief as well. Or you may have the limiting beliefs that people with money change for the worst and you don't want to be that person.

Having these self-limiting beliefs can be based on your past experiences or they arise because of a fear of a future event. These can be fears of failure, criticism, or financial loss. The key is to understand that you have them and before you move forward with your goals and outcomes, you must learn to eliminate or reduce their effect upon you. Only then, will you move forward with your transformation towards success and freedom. So, think about what limiting beliefs you may have at this time. This is an important step, so take the time to analyze any limiting beliefs that could be holding you back.

You will go through an exercise that will help you identify your own limiting beliefs. Once you do, I will have you write them down, so be prepared with a journal or pen and paper.

For this and the remaining exercises, you can download worksheets by going to:

https://www.docdeliversbooks.com/free-ebook/

Scroll down the page to find the appropriate one for the exercise, titled "Limiting Beliefs."

How do we know we have them?

So, to determine your own limiting beliefs, you're going to focus on some key verbal attributes, physical attributes, and emotional attributes that will signal that you have them.

For this step, you are going to look at yourself from the third person perspective. Relax your mind and imagine you are sitting in an empty theater watching the movie of your life on the screen. What's even cooler about this theater is that not only can we hear and see what's on the screen, but we can also feel the emotions and sensations that go with it.

Now, the movie is about to play, and you see yourself starting to talk about your life and some of the challenges that you may have encountered in recent times. As you are watching and listening to your character speak, pay attention to some of these words that represent a limiting belief. For example, think about the last time you tried a new skill or didn't succeed at the goal that you set for yourself.

Are you telling yourself:

"I *don't* ..."

"I *can't* ..."

"I *won't* ..."

"I don't, can't or won't *because* ..."

When you notice using these language pattern in the future, understand that this is a limiting belief that you have regarding that event or situation.

Some physical symptoms that you may be experiencing with regards to your limited beliefs could be things, such as:

Feeling your stomach get upset and getting nauseous as you are thinking about, talking about, or trying to attempt doing a task.

Feeling your heart rate rise at the mere mention of an event.

Breaking into a cold sweat as you try to attempt doing a task.

This also taps into the third and final attribute that can give us a clue if you have a limiting belief regarding a situation. Emotional states are powerful triggers that can give you strong clues regarding your own limiting beliefs.

For example, you may have an overwhelming fear of trying to achieve a goal or an obstacle. Many times, it's not the **physical action** of doing something that triggers your fear but it's simply the **thought process** that overwhelms and cripples you. Apprehension and nervousness are other emotional states that will indicate that you have a limiting belief as well.

So how did you get your limiting beliefs?

Your limiting beliefs in life have been developed and continue to grow because of your experiences. Interactions with your family or friends, being in the classroom setting with fellow students or teachers; your daily interactions in life are just some of the ways that your limiting beliefs are created and enforced.

Now these beliefs don't start as thought patterns that you accept without question. They often start as simple suggestions, opinions, or situations that you may have consciously or subconsciously decided to explore further. But as these events continue to stack upon one another, they reinforce the original suggestion, opinion, or situation into one that is more solidified and harder to break.

And as time continues to go on, your verbal, physical and emotional cues become so automatic that you start to accept these limiting beliefs as your current reality.

But understand this, your limiting beliefs are exactly what they are:

Beliefs.

Acknowledging your own limiting beliefs

So right now, I want you to get your journal and write down two limiting beliefs that you have. It doesn't have to be perfect or the ones you think are the worst. Just putting down two on paper will be a powerful exercise to start the process of really seeing how these beliefs affect your life. Make sure you have space between the two because the next step is to answer these four questions for each one.

Here are the series of questions:

1. Who, other than myself, is affected by this belief?

2. How long have I had this belief?

3. What is this belief costing me?

4. Why do I choose to believe it?

When you complete these questions, you're going to begin to realize the physical, mental, spiritual, and emotional cost that you are paying by hanging onto them.

This worksheet is available at:

https://www.docdeliversbooks.com/free-ebook/

When there, scroll down to the section called "Limiting Beliefs."

Got them written down? Nice!

How was that exercise for you?

Did you gain some insight into how your limiting beliefs have been holding you back, robbing you of achieving the full potential to move towards the goals and outcomes that you desire? Seeing how your own beliefs hold you back is a good thing because now you see what needs to be addressed in order to move forward productively.

Next, let's look at the timing of your self-limiting beliefs. Are they based on something that has happened in the past or something that you fear in the future? What's great for you is that you absolutely can move forward despite what has happened in the past. You also can move forward despite your feelings about the future because those feelings are based on something that you assume. It's not based on an actual event because it hasn't happened yet. With a small shift in your thinking, you will begin to realize that you have the power to do and create great things!

These questions may annoy or anger you and if so, good! It's about time we hit a nerve and cracked through that hard outer shell of your beliefs. Now with the limiting beliefs in front of you, let's work on rewording them.

Reversing the language of your limiting beliefs

For this part, you are going to use some sneaky tactics to gradually replace your limiting belief statement with one that your mind can readily accept now. The reason that your limiting belief is so easy for you to accept is because it's **comfortable** for your mind to accept.

Tweaking your current limiting beliefs in a way that's comfortable for your mind to accept will serve you in a more positive way.

Here is a recap of some the limiting beliefs that were identified earlier:

"I don't have enough time in the day to do what I truly desire."

"Since I have failed in the past, I will probably fail at the next thing that I do."

"You have to be smart in order to make money."

One of the most powerful things about limiting beliefs is that they are worded as absolutes. They are structured in a way that encompasses everything, making your mind feel comfortable and not allowing you the opportunity to escape it.

So, here is the key to escape the belief:

Start using language that is not absolute. It's simple!

To turn a self-limiting belief into a self-motivating belief, think of your language as a 12-inch ruler and your goal is to gradually move your language from self-limiting (one or two inches) gradually up to 12.

You don't want to pull a superman move and make a single leap all the way to 12. Your conscious and subconscious mind won't accept that right away. You are going to take small steps that don't trigger the panic button of your mind, allowing it to still feel safe and without fear.

Here's one example for changing self-limiting beliefs:

"I don't have enough time in the day to do what I truly desire."

Are you saying 24 hours a day, seven days a week, you have absolutely no time for yourself?

Let's change the self-limiting statement just a little bit. Here is an example of changing your language from an absolute statement towards one that creates a possibility:

"My time may be limited some days but there are others when I can do the things to accomplish what I desire."

Now you are shifting your thoughts from an impossibility towards something that is possible!

Let's look at another example:

"Since I have failed in the past, I will probably fail at the next thing that I do."

Failure is nothing more than an opportunity to learn. You found one way that didn't work so now you are closer towards discovering what does. So, a way to change this language would be:

"I have learned from my failures in the past so now I can avoid those mistakes in the next thing that I do."

Finally, there is the statement:

"You have to be smart in order to make money."

There are countless people who have made money who were not the best in their class. There are many more factors beyond intelligence that will assist you with making the income that you desire. One way to reframe this would be:

"I have the creativity to figure out how to make more money."

Overall, reframing your self-limiting beliefs will help you make the transition towards seeing the possibility in your actions. Having more of a positive mindset will help empower you to take the necessary steps towards achieving the goals and outcomes that you desire.

Conclusion of limiting beliefs

Practice and have fun with rewording your limiting beliefs. As you start to do it more often, you will come to realize how powerful changing one or two words can be!

In time, you will potentially discover new limiting beliefs and reword them in a way that's more positive and productive. As you continue to develop, those reworded beliefs will help accelerate your journey towards what you desire.

From now on, you will call these new limiting beliefs simply "empowering beliefs," eliminating as much of the negative connotation that is associated with them.

With the first tool of understanding and busting your limiting beliefs complete, now it's time to develop a powerful "why" for you.

CHAPTER 5
DISCOVERING YOUR "WHY"

Discovering your why is probably the most crucial step that will help you determine who is the person that you wish to be at this stage in your life. There are many people that say why they wish to do something, however, they do it on a very superficial level and don't dig deep enough.

We can understand that we may want to be a more joyful or happy or loving person and that is a wonderful way to start; however, it is very superficial because it's simply not powerful enough. What you are going to do right now is develop a powerful "WHY" for yourself, which will enhance the person that you wish to be.

What you are going to do at this point is start with your why and eventually go seven levels deep.

Why are you doing this?

Because if I can help build a more powerful "why" statement for you, something that resonates with your soul and your core, it's going to become so powerful that it makes the person that you wish to be more effective, focused, and in the end, more successful.

So, here's an example of going seven levels deep.

I'm going to use my own journey in life as an example so that it can give you more clarity on the power of "why" and how it enhances the person that I wish to be. For me, the person that I wished to be was happier and more joyful. This example is just to help you understand the process of going seven levels deep. My "why" statement reflects a desire to help people better understand themselves through this book.

Your why statement would reflect why you wish to achieve the goals and outcomes that you desire.

Having a "why" statement of, "I wanted to be more happy and joyful," is too superficial and generic. I needed to have a why statement that was more powerful. When I would read the why statement to myself, it needed to be one that would drive me, despite the obstacles and challenges. So, what I will show you and what you will do later in this chapter is reveal the transition from a superficial and generic statement towards one that is powerful and transformational.

When I asked myself why I wanted to be a mentor, life coach and entrepreneur, my first "why" statement was, "I wanted to be more happy and joyful." The key to making the most powerful statement is by continuing to ask yourself why you believe it. You do this repetitively, digging deeper to a more powerful and meaningful statement. After asking myself "Why?" six more times, I finally came up with the statement that I needed. In the end, my why statement became, "As more people become inspired, they will learn anything and everything that they desire is possible and I will feel fulfilled that my efforts helped make the world a better place for my family and loved ones."

Can you see the difference between the original and final why statements? The final reveals the positive impact that I desire for my world and family. That resonates with me as the journey towards my goals and outcomes gets tough. My statement drives me forward because my goals and outcomes are much bigger than me personally. It's about helping as many people get the dreams that they desire.

So, let's look at the process of digging seven levels deep so you have a guide to develop your own powerful statement.

The answer to my original question of why I wanted to be a coach and entrepreneur was wanting to be happier and more joyful.

Then I asked myself a second why: "Why do I want to be more happy and joyful?"

The answer to this question was, "I wished to live a life that felt more fulfilling and exciting!"

Then I asked myself a third why: "Why do I wish to feel more fulfilled and excited?"

My answer: "I wish to share my passion and excitement with others to inspire them."

"Why do I wish to inspire others?" was the fourth why I asked myself.

"I wish to inspire others to understand that small shifts in their mindset can help them move forward."

The next why question that I asked myself was, "Why do I wish to help people move forward?"

"I want to help people move forward so that they could discover that they are truly capable of achieving anything and everything that they desire in life."

The next question I asked was, "Why do I wish to help people achieve what they desire?"

"Because as more people become successful with their own lives, they in turn inspire others to do the same."

The seventh and final why that I asked myself was: "Why is inspiring other people to inspire others important to me?"

"As more people become inspired, they will learn anything and everything that they desire is possible and I will feel fulfilled that my efforts helped make the world a better place for my family and loved ones."

Going back to my original why statement, I answered that I wished to be happier and more joyful. However, I enhanced this with a more powerful and deeper why. Knowing that I will leave this world a better place to live resonates so much more powerfully with me.

It puts me in a state of being that constantly reminds me that the person I wish to be is not only benefiting myself but is benefiting the world around me. With this one-two combination of the BE and the WHY, it's essentially a knockout blow for my success within the Circle of Conception (coming up next)!

Can you see the power of asking yourself "why" seven levels deep can transform you into the person that you wish to be more effectively?

I thought you would!

You can download the "Why" exercise worksheets at:

https://www.docdeliversbooks.com/free-ebook/

and scroll down to the section called "Discover Your Why and Be."

Once you learn who you wish to be, and combine that with a powerful why statement, you will be an unstoppable force, achieving all that you desire in your life!

If at this point you feel stuck on who you wish to be, or you truly just don't know the answer, here are some common questions that you can ask yourself to help jumpstart the thought process for you.

What was my reason for purchasing this book?

What am I passionate about in my life right now?

What's important to me?

If I had a magic potion to wake up with everything that I wanted in life, how would life be different?

How would completing this book enhance my life?

What do I really want and desire in life?

What inspires and motivates me to keep going?

Right now, I want you to take some time to write about who that person you wish to be is. It doesn't need to be very complex and I want you to make it very simple with just one sentence. You are building a simplified foundation for your "be."

I want you to write down the first thing that comes to mind because often your first thoughts are more accurate. I don't want you to overthink too deeply at this stage because I want you to use more of your gut and your core feelings to help establish the person that you wish to be.

Did you complete the exercise?

Again, to have your "why" and "be" statements together, checkout the download page at:

https://www.docdeliversbooks.com/free-ebook/

and scroll down to the section called "Discover Your Why and Be."

By having a better understanding of the person you wish to be, you will develop your own seven levels deep why statements.

Remember, this is something that I want you to take the time to really dive into. You need to develop a powerful "why" that will resonate so deeply with your core, it will have a profound effect on the person that you wish to be. Having a powerful "why" will jumpstart the person that you wish to be and allow you to move along the Circle of Conception more effectively by enhancing your commitment, engagement, and actions.

Take the next 20 minutes to develop your seven levels deep questions that will enhance the person who you wish to be.

Are you complete?

Excellent!

Let's recap what we have learned in level one, otherwise known as your foundation. Your first tool was to understand limiting beliefs and learn how to change the language pattern to break them. Second, you developed a powerful "why" that empowered you to strive even harder towards the person that you wish to be.

So, what is the value of taking these two prenatal vitamins before moving onto phase two, the "Circle of Conception?"

Before starting the next level, you needed to have the **foundation** of having a mindset that would support and encourage you to move forward. Minimizing and eliminating your limiting beliefs starts the process of believing that change is possible, and it's reinforced with having a powerful why that will strengthen it.

Have your written "beliefs" and "seven levels deep" exercises handy so you can reflect upon it when you experience setbacks and roadblocks during your journey to delivering an enhanced version of yourself.

We all have pitfalls in life but having these two tools, especially a powerful "why," will give you the ammunition and motivation to keep forging forward!

At this time, I would like to congratulate you for completing your preconception care and level one of the process!

Next stop in your journey towards delivering an enhanced version of you is the start of level two: Focus

SECTION 3
Level 2: Focus

CHAPTER 6
UNDERSTANDING YOUR "CIRCLE OF CONCEPTION"

Level two is called "Focus" because you will focus on developing the skills that will let you flow towards achieving your goals and outcomes. As you continue to learn the strategies that will get you the goals that you desire, you will experience growth and transformation. Think of this development like the trimesters of pregnancy, with each one building upon the previous level. Like a newborn who needs to develop over 40 weeks, you will develop and build upon the skills that will get you what you desire in life.

The reason I describe this as a "circle" is because life is not about hitting a goal and calling it a day. Life is about continuing to grow and improve upon the gains that you have made. Like the circle, life is a never-ending loop of constant growth. Once you achieve the goals that you desire, I know you won't be satisfied with them. You will have the mindset that anything and everything is possible. Thus, you will continue your journey to further transform yourself.

We previously discussed the concept of:

See and act were the missing components that are done by successful people. Each step, from be to have, must be in this specific order because one concept builds upon the next. It's like the growth of a newborn. Each stage, the first, second and third trimesters, builds upon the previous one, eventually delivering a bundle of joy, later providing the aftercare to keep them healthy. You will go through a transformation as well, developing the skills that are needed to help deliver the goals and outcomes that you desire.

Here is a quick overview of the stages.

The first trimester will focus on:

BE – This stage focuses upon the development of your core values and growing mentally. Here, you will get additional tools that will put you in a mindset of confidence and success.

The second trimester will focus on:

DO – Building upon the previous trimester, now you are mentally prepared to do the **internal actions** that will help you overcome the fears in your life. You will identify your fears and I will provide you with the tools to *mentally* overcome them.

The third trimester will focus on:

SEE – Here, you will learn techniques of visualization to see yourself **now** as the person that you will **become** in the future. Because you have developed a mindset for success and overcome your fears in the second trimester, seeing your future success will be easier!

Your rebirth will focus on:

ACT – All the trimesters prepared you for this stage. Now it's time to execute the **external actions** that will move you even closer towards the goals and outcomes that you desire. You will learn how to take action that is specific, time efficient and productive for what you desire. Your external actions will *physically* push you past your fears.

Your post conception care will focus on:

HAVE – You are well on the way towards your goals and outcomes, moving efficiently and effectively. Things are new and exciting for you. Looking at newborns when they come back to my office, I see them constantly looking around, taking in the sights and sounds of their new environment and it's an exciting time for them (well, they may not understand the concept of excitement, but they feel it)! Now, it's your time to explore your new mindset and environment. It's a time for reflection on what you have now and what can be done to enhance the new you even further. Thus, this section will focus on re-evaluating yourself for your further growth and development. Don't think that you will go through this process only once! Life is about constantly transforming yourself in positive ways.

CHAPTER 7
YOUR FIRST TRIMESTER: BE

You start with "BE", which is going to be the most detailed and essential component within the Circle of Conception, because it is the starting point of everything that you do. If your "BE" is not established, your chances of completing this essential circle are going to be extremely minimized.

Think of it in this way:

You have a brand-new shiny sports car that is top-of-the-line and the envy of all your family and friends. Now imagine this car has unlimited mileage and carrying capacity so that you can go anywhere that you desire in life and take all the necessary things that you need for your journey.

The car is delivered to your front door brand-new, all its components are explained to you in detail, and you are handed over the keys to start your journey. However, the one thing that you forgot to do before you started your travels was to fill your car with gas.

You were so excited about receiving the car, packing it with all the things that you needed for your trip. However, in all of your excitement, you forgot to add the most critical component to make it work. It was a simple oversight because of your enthusiasm and joy for being able to drive to the next destination in life that you desired.

But without the gas in the car, it is basically an expensive concept that has nowhere to go.

Think of your "BE" as the gas.

If you try to move forward in your life and you don't provide it with the proper fuel to get it going, you're going to be at a standstill. So, you're going to optimize the fuel that you need to get you moving forward. So, what is the fuel that will help you become the person that you desire, achieving the goals and outcomes that you want? The fuel involves developing your core values and having a mindset with more focus.

The importance of core values is very simple. They are the beliefs that you have about yourself, guiding your thoughts, beliefs, and actions towards the person who you wish to be. They are the elements guiding how you live your life day to day, for better or for worse. Having core values of being selfish or arrogant will significantly limit your options to grow in a productive way. On the other hand, compassion and determination would be core values that will fuel you towards any future destination that you desire.

Focus is the other critical piece needed for becoming who you desire. It involves having the right mindset that enhances your chances for success. Focus on being broke and you will struggle to have positive thoughts for obtaining financial abundance. Focus on abundance and you open your mind to more creativity and ideas for achieving financial success.

Developing Your Core

There are many people that don't understand what their core values are or what they feel is a vital component of themselves. It also may be something that you truly have not defined in the past. You will identify the values within your life and then consolidate them into three or four "core" values. These will be the foundation for becoming the person that you are or simply your "BE." Understand that the way that you talk, think, and act reflects your core values. Identifying them will be your guide towards figuring out what works in your life, what doesn't work and what you need to make it better.

Some of the questions that you can ask yourself to determine your core values would be the following:

What are some characteristic or traits that I have which are important to me?

If I were to ask how others see me, what would be one word that they would say that described me?

What is the image that I wish to portray to others?

When I think about a time in my life that was special or outstanding for me, how did I see myself, what were some of these things that were said to me, or how did I feel?

When I had times in my life when things didn't work out the way that I was expecting them to, what would have been an opposite emotion of what I was feeling at that time?

Here is a list of values that you can use as a guide to help you. As you look at the list, see which core values you identify with. The goal is to create a list of at least 20 core values, but no more than 30:

Ambitious	Assertive	Aware	Approachable	Altruistic	Amusing
Bold	Balanced	Brave	Brilliant	Beneficent	Beautiful
Competitive	Calm	Capable	Courageous	Confident	Consistent
Dedicated	Decisive	Dominant	Determined	Driven	Disciplined
Empathetic	Efficient	Educated	Enthusiastic	Entertaining	Ethical
Faithful	Friendly	Flexible	Fun	Fearless	Firm
Giving	Grateful	Good-willed	Graceful	Growing	Generous
Honest	Healthy	Humble	Humorous	Hard-working	Happy
Innovative	Independent	Imaginative	Inquisitive	Integrity	Intelligent
Joyful	Just				
Kind	Keen	Knowledgeable			
Loving	Listener	Loyal	Logical	Level-headed	Leader
Motivated	Mature	Mellow	Meticulous	Modest	Mysterious
Neat	Nice	Nimble	Noble		
Optimistic	Open	Ordered	Obedient	Original	Outrageous
Precise	Prepared	Punctual	Private	Punctual	Professional
Quick	Quiet	Quality			
Relaxed	Realistic	Resourceful	Resolve	Respectful	Resilient
Selfless	Silly	Speedy	Successful	Smart	Sympathetic
Team-player	Timely	Transparent	Tough	Thankful	Trustworthy
Unique	Understanding	Unstoppable	Useful		
Vigorous	Virtuous	Visionary			
Wise	Willpower	Welcoming			
Zestful					

You can download the list and 3-step worksheets by going to:

https://www.docdeliversbooks.com/free-ebook/

and scroll down to the section called "Core Values."

So, you should have a list of 20 to 30 values and now you're going to consolidate this list down to four to five "core values." This will make it more manageable and easier to remember.

For example, you may have several values such as hard-working, resilient, sustainability, and persistence; perhaps the common theme among these four words could be sustainability?

The next step is to look at the four or five core values that you have developed and then turn them into a powerful statement for each one. You are going to create statements that invoke emotion and power, enhancing the person that you wish to be.

Using our previous example of sustainability, you may have a statement such as the following:

"The sustainability that I have in my life enhances me each and every day."

Now you are going to do that with each of your core values, turning them into the four or five statements that you read to yourself every day.

Why are you doing this?

Well first, to reinforce and remind you of who you wish to be.

Second, you are creating micro habits that will help develop your unconscious thoughts and actions. Outdated theories say that it takes 21 days to form a new habit. I'm going to even make it less challenging for you, but it will still be as powerful. For the next seven days, I require you to read this statement to yourself each day. It can be in the morning or afternoon or evening, the time is up to you. Now you may think this is silly but if you cannot do something as simple as read these four or five core value statements to yourself for seven days, how do you expect to be able to do the harder challenges to get the outcomes that you desire?

Your list of core values represents your "core value statements." Reflecting upon them every day will remind you of your strengths.

Remember, you are building a mindset of repetition in order to develop your unconscious thinking into a pattern of success. This is way more important than giving you a blueprint for your actions and outcomes immediately. You are building the foundation of your core, reinforcing your "BE" which in turn, creates a mindset within your subconscious for success.

Understand this, there is nothing more critical to your success than the way that you talk to yourself.

Your language pattern is everything and the language that you have within yourself, how you communicate consciously, gets embedded within your subconscious. So, if you have conscious statements that reflect your positive core values, you are subconsciously going to become more of the person that you wish to be.

Again, language is everything and how you do anything is how you do everything. Think of it in this way:

If you ate junk food or fast food all-day long, what would be the result? Would you have the optimal physique that you desired, or would you be overweight, sluggish, or even have suboptimal health?

If you ate healthy food more often than not, do you think your chances for having a healthier lifestyle would be enhanced?

That is the state that I wish to get your subconscious into. Having positive thoughts more often than not is key. Because 95% of your actions are based on subconscious thoughts, internalizing strong core values sets you up for success.

When you start that first week of stating your core value statements every day, take the time to congratulate yourself! Don't wait until the end before giving yourself credit for your success. Develop the mindset that success is not an endpoint, but it is a journey that is celebrated along the way.

As you complete each week, you're going to celebrate the fact that you took the simple steps today that will result in your transformation. As you resonate with your core values now, you will enhance them, moving closer towards the person who you truly wish to be.

Again, you can download the worksheet to do all three steps at:

https://www.docdeliversbooks.com/free-ebook/ at "core values."

Identifying Your Focus

We briefly discussed mindset and its importance in getting the goals and outcomes that you desire. Expanding upon it, having the proper mindset involves enhancing the level of communication that you have with yourself.

If you found yourself struggling with trying to complete the previous exercise and develop your four or five core value statements, the issue is probably not that you lack positive core values, but the issue might be the thoughts that you have about yourself.

The thoughts that you have about yourself go beyond the simplicity of having positive thoughts or negative thoughts. It may seem simple or completely clear, however I'm still going to touch upon this. Obviously, when you have thoughts that are positive about yourselves, such as feeling happy or confident, they set you up for a higher chance of achieving your desired outcomes in life. And when you have thoughts, such as failure, sadness, or disappointment, it's going to make it more prone that you're not as successful because you don't have the proper mindset, or state that sets you up for success.

Again, it goes beyond the simple thought process of thinking positively or negatively.

In addition to positive or negative thoughts, focus also involves the time frame where your thoughts occur. Is the time frame of your thoughts set in the past, present, or future?

Continuing with the theme of a negative thought process, these may be some of the questions that you need to ask yourself:

Do you believe that your actions today are a result of events that happened in the **past**?

Do you think that your **present** actions today are a result of not having clarity in your life? Not understanding how to move forward towards what you desire?

Do you think the way that you act prohibits you from moving forward towards your desired **future** outcomes because they feel unattainable or unrealistic?

These are questions that focus on having that negative mindset that's attached to the past, present, or future.

Enhancing your focus also involves you asking the right questions to yourself. Because when you ask yourself the right questions, you will soon realize the true language that you are feeding to your subconscious. If that language is negative, you're going to begin to ask the questions that will help reinforce a positive mindset, and thus refocus your subconscious thoughts for automated success.

Here are the four critical questions that you must ask yourself in order to start the process of discovery, retooling your mindset for positive thoughts and success:

1. What PLEASURE do I gain by NOT going for the dreams that I desire?

2. What PAIN do I gain by going for the dreams that I desire?

3. What PAIN do I gain by NOT going for the dreams that I desire?

4. What PLEASURE do I gain by going for the dreams that I desire?

Now, let's breakdown each of these questions to provide you with more clarity. Let's use the example of trying to lose weight.

When you look at the first question, "What PLEASURE do I gain by NOT going for the dreams that I desire?" The pleasure that you gain may be that you get to eat anything at any time of the day and can feel good about doing so.

When you look at the second question, "What PAIN do I gain by going for the dreams that I desire?" The pain that you gain is that you may be sore from workouts or tired of eating foods that you usually don't eat.

Looking at the third question, "What PAIN do I gain by NOT going for the dreams that I desire?" The pain that you may experience is that as you get unhealthier, you're not as physically active, or may have to take more medications because of the medical problems that you're developing.

And finally, the last question is, "What PLEASURE do I gain by going for the dreams that I desire?" You're living a healthier lifestyle that allows you to be more active with the family, have less stress, and have more energy to do the things in life that are desired.

When you reread and answer each one of these questions, it will give you a glimpse into your mindset and tell you what your driving force is behind what you do or don't do. *Are you more driven by pleasure or are you more driven by pain?*

Looking at the last two questions, it may become more obvious to you that you may have more success in achieving your outcome when you truly look at the pain that is involved when you fail at the task. Like in our example, the pain of living an unhealthy lifestyle that may take you away from your family, friends and loved ones prematurely can drive you towards the pleasure of the positive outcomes that you will achieve once the task is completed.

Looking at the first two questions, you may have the mindset that the pleasure of inactivity is more satisfying to you than the pain of trying to achieve the outcome.

There are no correct answers for these four questions and they depend on your outcome in your situation. It's simply to help you explore what may be holding you back from achieving the goals and outcomes that you desire.

Once you realize this, you will begin to ask yourself the questions and you'll determine if you are the type of person that is either:

Driven by pleasure *or*…

Driven by pain.

Many people are wired within their brains to be driven by pain, which is why you see them trying to work towards their outcomes when they are absolutely forced to do so. For example, you may see the overweight person start to take a serious look at their health, exercise, and diet after having a life-changing event, like a heart attack. In the other direction, you may see the person take a serious look at their health, exercise, and diet because they are driven by the pleasure of having the beach body that they desire in the upcoming summer.

If you are the type of person that is driven by pain or pleasure, these four questions will help you determine that. You will start to develop the right mindset and ask the questions that will move you in the right direction. Being driven by pain may be seen by some as a negative thing, but I disagree. If your pain is strong enough to give you incentive to drive towards your goals, then go for it! There is so much information out there that you must have a positive mindset to get what you want. Being in a positive mindset 100% of the time can be challenging. Thus, use pain to your advantage and let it fuel and motivate you towards the person that you wish to be.

Reinforcing Your "BE" and Establishing Your "STATE"

One of the important steps in enhancing the person that you wish to be is by utilizing what I call "future pacing." It is speaking, acting, and visualizing yourself **now** as the person that you wish to be in the **future**.

One of the powerful techniques that will assist you with this is when you get to "SEE" or visualize your success.

Simply, you will learn to "be," and more importantly, "act" as the person that you desire to be now.

You previously established your core values and have listed the ones that most resonate with you. They represent the person that you wish to grow into, enhance, and eventually become.

Are these values ones that you will grow into, enhancing your life?

If you say no and you feel that there is not room or a need for improvement, then I would challenge you to reconsider the values that you selected. The key is to challenge yourself and grow into someone bigger, an enhanced version of you.

For example, if you have a core value of honesty and you truly believe that you are honest with the people around you (and even more importantly, yourself), then consider a value that can serve you even more. Not to say that honesty isn't important, but you are looking to "grow" and get uncomfortable with core values that will enhance the ones that are strong already.

So, you may ask, "What is the importance of establishing a strong set of core values?" There are several reasons why:

The "external you"

Enhancing your ability to socially interact with others depends on the core values that resonate within you. You may describe yourself as an introvert, and even with this label that you put upon yourself, social interactions are more valuable than you may realize.

You socially interact with your spouse, significant other, family members or friends. You are creating connections of harmony, trust, and love with those around you.

You socially interact with co-workers or those that you have business connections with. They are optimized as you develop the necessary connections to be proficient and effective at work.

You socially interact with people that you meet for the first time. Even with a first-time meeting, people will gain an impression of you, deciding whether they like you or not within a matter of seconds.

Why is this important?

Have you noticed in your interactions with others that some are pleasant and others are downright toxic?

The reason is that the core values that you currently have are reflected in your external being. For example, having a core value of confidence will be seen immediately to the people that you work with and if you had a lack of self-confidence, others may be less hesitant to work with you or may simply not trust or value your opinions or words.

What image of yourself do you desire to project?

The "internal you"

This is a combination of several components which will provide a foundation for your core values. Having identified, written down and moved along the path of your core values, your ability to successfully maintain and enhance them will depend upon the five core states you could be in.

They are your emotional state, your thinking state, your action state, your learning state and finally, your playful state.

Why is it important to recognize what state you are in? Because when you find yourself off track from your goals and outcomes, knowing what state you are in will help you self-correct.

    1. Your emotional state.

What is the emotion that you have right now? Is there acceptance of what you are reading or are you feeling resistant or skeptical?

Your emotional state is going to help drive your success because having positive emotions such as joy, happiness, or inspiration will move you towards what you desire.

2. Your thinking state.

This is a continuation of your emotional state because it represents the internal communication that you have with yourself. Say for example, you have a negative emotional state of fear, worry, or doubt which triggers the verbal communication within you. You may start to manifest the communication within that "this is too overwhelming" or "I don't know how to pull this off."

However, an emotional state of joy or inspiration, will lay the seeds of internal communication that will fuel you with thoughts such as, "I can and will do this," or "I'm feeling confident I can take the first step."

The thinking state becomes the platform for the next step, your action state.

3. Your action state.

Your internal emotions will trigger your internal thoughts, which in turn, drive the actions that you do or don't do. Action is the key towards stepping into the core values that you desire and eventually, the goals and outcomes that you seek. Starting with a state of joy or optimism that triggers the communication of "I can be successful," will provide you with the initial motivation and confidence to take that first step of action.

For example, let's say that you have a core value of discipline. Your desired goal is to lose 20 pounds in three months with the outcome of having a healthier and fitter you.

You may start with an **emotional state** of enthusiasm, which leads to…

A **thinking state** of, "I'm feeling energized and ready to become a healthier version of me," which leads to…

An **action state** of having the discipline to eat healthy three days a week, starting right now, leading to…

An enhanced chance of successfully achieving your goal, which in turn…

Allows you to achieve the outcome that you desire, becoming the future person that you have envisioned.

Understand this, one state is a platform for the success or failure of the next, so all five of these states are critically important.

Remember…

Your core values will help you define and achieve the goals and outcomes that you desire.

    4. Your learning state.

The learning state is important because it allows you to reflect upon three powerful self-reflection questions. These are key questions to ask yourself because it will allow you to self-assess your progress along your path of stepping into your core values. So, as you travel your path and attempt to grow into the core values that you desire, ask yourself:

    a. What am I doing right?

    b. What am I doing not so right?

    c. How can I make it better?

Notice I didn't say, "What am I doing wrong" for the second question. It's not by accident because the key is to develop a mindset where everything that you try and do is a learning opportunity.

In his quest to develop the first lightbulb, Thomas Edison went through multiple trials before finally succeeding at his creation. He was famously asked by a reporter, "How did it feel to fail 1000 times?" He simply replied, "I didn't fail a thousand times. The lightbulb was an invention with a thousand steps."

What if Edison saw himself as a failure after the first 10 attempts, or the 100th, or even attempt #999?

Everything that you do is the opportunity to self-reflect and grow yourself. Stop thinking about failure and start thinking about focusing and forging forward. It's how I approach the way I look at my core values, goals, or outcomes.

For me, I don't have days when I fail. I do have challenging days and I reflect upon these three powerful questions to keep moving me forward in the direction that best serves me.

    5. The fun state.

This is a state that I am working on the most right now!

Over the years, I have developed a level of professionalism with my colleagues and patients, optimizing my social interactions and level of medical care.

However, somewhere along the way, I forgot how to have fun! And because of this, combined with my intense emotional state of determination, I forged forward but inhibited my overall growth. I didn't take the time to "stop and smell the roses."

Life is not about a start and finish line.

It's about a journey, one that you must learn to appreciate and have fun along the way. Now, I'm not saying to go out and throw a party every time you hit one of your targets along the way (unless you want to!) but I am saying to simply smile, reflect upon, and acknowledge the progress that you have made. Not everyone has the courage to design an enhanced version of themselves, so be happy, grateful, and have fun knowing that you are on this wonderful journey for yourself!

How to start *being* more now

You are about to dive in towards the "three versions of yourself," but before you do, let's have a final conversation on the importance of future pacing your "being." Essentially, future pacing is imagining your future self as the person that you are today. It's a powerful tool that you will get to play with when you get to the section called "SEE."

For now, let's touch upon some of the important reasons why "Being" the future version of yourself is critical to everything else that you do.

Gratitude

Now, don't expect to be grateful for what you have in life and wake up the next day with a million dollars. It simply doesn't work that way. However, when you are grateful for what you have, be it your health, family, finances, friends, and so on, you are doing a few things.

First, you are creating a positive mindset which is essential for optimizing your core values, goals, and outcomes. Second, you begin to expand your vision.

I will touch on this in a minute because it flows nicely into the second reason why you should "BE" the future you.

Law of Attraction

Again, another of those concepts that everyone and their mama talks about! As you begin to have gratitude for where you are at now, it opens the door for receiving or having the situations, opportunities, or events that you need along your path of becoming an enhanced version of you.

Have you ever wondered why some people seem to have everything go their way? Opportunities just seem to fall in their lap without any effort at all.

It's not because some people are simply more blessed and favored in this world.

It's because people with a mindset of gratitude SEE the opportunities that they need, and you don't.

If you are in a positive mindset of gratitude, you will begin to realize things that were already in your life as opportunities that you can use moving it forward. It's your positive mindset which allows you to become more aware, focusing on what you need, enhancing your ability to see it.

I remember buying a brand-new SUV, a Lincoln Navigator, and the feeling of joy for having a nice car that I was excited about driving around in. I felt so special because I believed that I was in a special place by having a quality vehicle.

Guess what happened a few weeks later? I started seeing people drive Lincoln Navigators all over the place!

Was it that there was a mad rush of Navigators being sold or was it that my perception of them already out there became more focused?

Tricking your subconscious mind!

Again, this will be explained in more detail as we get to the "SEE" section. Are you noticing a theme that the "SEE" section is really going to be powerful for you?

What the mind visualizes and accepts as reality, will be reflected in your conscious state. If you believe you are a failure and can never get a break, guess what, breaks won't come your way!

If you believe you are successful and worthy of success, then you will begin to discover that life unfolds towards the mindset that you have implanted within your subconsciousness.

"Whatever the mind can conceive and believe, the mind can achieve."
– Napoleon Hill

We will train your mind later to develop powerful visualizations, so detailed and realistic, that your mind will accept it as reality.

You are what you feel

For some, it may be difficult and challenging to step into core values that may not be congruent with the way that they are living today. For example, you may have a core value that you want to be more confident, however, your current being is shy and withdrawn. So how do you start to step towards achieving congruency with who you desire to be and who you are now?

Again, it's visualization (again!!!) but for now understand this:

As you start to see yourself NOW as the person that you wish to become, it allows you to slowly build the confidence, develop the possibilities of how the enhanced version of you is. You begin to see the more confident you, talking to people who once intimidated you. You begin to feel the joy of opening up to others in conversation. Your internal language shifts from one of doubt to one of optimism.

It's the reason why this, and all the other ones (Gratitude, Law of Attraction, Tricking Your Subconscious) are important. When you begin to mentally act as the person that you desire to be later, you start the process of becoming that person right now.

I future pace myself every day, setting myself up for success as each day goes by. Each evening, I relax and get into a state where I visualize myself the next day as the person that I wish to be. I see and believe that I am the determined, disciplined, and confident man *now* that I see as my future self.

It will take some time to mentally, emotionally, and physically accept this, but you will begin to realize that, with enough time and practice, it will be automatic and effortless for you.

As one of my mentors says, "You are going to be crappy at it first then you will begin to get better."

Take the time and open your mind to the possibilities of seeing an enhanced version of you.

Again, we will expand upon visualization and future pacing in the upcoming chapters, but I needed to first get you into a state of thinking outside the box, understanding the importance of your core values and seeing yourself now as the person that you wish to become.

Understanding your goals and outcomes

So, let's recap the journey that we have been on so far!

- Understanding **"why"** you *chose* to start this journey of overcoming your fears, conceiving your dreams, and delivering an enhanced version of yourself.

- Discovering and owning the **core values** that determine the person who you wish to become once your goals and outcomes are realized.

- Identifying different states that you will mentally and physically exist in, which is a reality check of where you are now, defining how successful you can be.

- Learning the initial concept of future pacing and how it benefits you by visualizing an enhanced version of yourself.

Pay attention, because this is the exciting portion of the journey which is creating the goals and outcomes that you desire. For now, I am going to provide you with an overview of how the system of breaking down your life into three specific outcomes works.

I need to do this now because I want you to get uncomfortable! The challenge here is to have you create outcomes for your life that stretch you, bringing you out of your little zone of comfort and security. In fact, I understand and welcome if this may be scary for you because the next major section will discuss fear and what you need to internally DO to overcome them.

That will be followed by visualization techniques that will have you optimize your success towards the initial outcomes that you will create now. After that, you will design the goals that are associated with your outcomes.

Let's briefly define outcomes and how I look at them differently from goals:

Your **outcome** is the state or person that you strive to be, such as a more successful business person, closer connection with a higher being, spouse or loved one.

Your **goals** are the waypoints along your journey to your outcomes.

Simplifying your life with three main outcomes

Over the years of creating personal goals and outcomes, I have tried many types of systems. But as I studied them more and more, I began to see a pattern that really simplified the process for me and in turn, it will be simple for you!

When I looked at my life and decided to create the outcomes (and later we will structure your goals around these) that best served me, I discovered that there are three main categories that encompass the vast majorities of outcomes that people can set for themselves.

They are the following:

Your personal self

Your social self

Your financial self

Most of the outcomes that you will create will fall into one of these three categories.

Having balance among your three selves

Now, you may have heard others state that "balance" is necessary in one's life, but exactly what does that mean?

Well, as I started my path towards entrepreneurship, growing into someone who would coach and mentor those who wanted to discover their own paths, I put all my energy into one single thing…

Growing my business at all costs.

Now, I am not knocking hard work, in fact, I support it because the harder you work, the more you fail, the greater you grow, the faster you know how to optimize your path for success. I remember many late nights working on social media, creating videos, writing blog content, keeping all the sites up to date, developing new teaching and coaching content and on and on. I became absorbed, no… *obsessed* with success, but it came at a cost. And that cost was my **personal** and **social** selves.

My **"financial"** self was growing but I was sacrificing my health and marriage.

I don't remember the exact trigger, but I soon came to realize that I could not sustain the pace of putting so much mental, physical, and emotional energy towards one component of my life.

It's kind of like trying to stay balanced on a three-legged chair that's missing one of the legs. Have you ever tried to do that (disclaimer: don't do it!). You are unsteady, unbalanced and, while you may be able to pull it off in the short term, you will fall off. And that fall will be HARD because you spent so much of your energy trying to stay upright.

Once I started balancing the personal, social, and financial, I began to realize and notice that I was MORE productive with the financial component. Why?

Because I was happier, had a ton more energy, and began to have the support of my wife, who resented me working so hard in the first place. Once she saw that she was a priority like everything else in my life, she provided me the mental and physical space to do what needed to be done.

Balance doesn't mean that you must divide all three of your outcome categories into equal parts. I'm not saying that at all. What I am saying is that you should have the mindset that you will provide some level of effort and focus on all of them. Somedays, I'm purely into the business. Others, I only focus on my wife and family and then there are days when I focus more on me!

However, I know that I constantly cycle among all versions of myself and knowing this, I become less stressed (as well as my wife!). Knowing that I don't have to go all-out for the business gives me that mental break, which is essential to recharge and reconnect with life outside business.

And the beauty of this system is that it's simplified, so I can focus on three categories of outcomes overall instead of having to worry about 15-20 different events.

Defining your three outcome categories for this system

As mentioned above, the three main categories that you will use as the basis for creating your outcomes are the following:

Your personal self

Your social self

Your financial self

So, what do these three things represent?

Your personal self

I start with defining your personal self because if you don't focus on developing a better you internally, it's going to be challenging to manifest the things that you want socially and financially.

It's almost as if you must take a selfish approach to life. But, this is exactly what is necessary in order to get an enhanced version of you. In turn, it will make those around you, your community, and your world that much better.

Have you ever flown on a commercial airline?

If you have, you are probably familiar with the safety talk and demonstration that is given by the flight attendants before the plane even takes off. Maybe you're not that familiar with it, as I notice that many people will tend to ignore these critical instructions.

They talk about the use of the seatbelts; the location of the emergency exits, and then they get into what I feel is the most important component of the entire discussion.

The oxygen masks.

The conversation goes somewhat like this:

The oxygen and the air pressure are always being monitored. In the event of a loss of cabin air pressure, an oxygen mask will drop from the compartment above your seat. To start the flow of oxygen, pull the mask towards you, fully extending the tube. Place it securely over your nose and mouth, with the elastic band behind your head and breathe normally. Although the bag is not inflated, oxygen is flowing to the mask. If you are traveling with a child or someone who requires assistance, secure your mask on first, and then assist the other person.

Now, the reason that I bring this up is because there was one critical line that is relevant to the discussion of enhancing your life. It is the line that talks about putting yourself first with regards to securing your mask.

*If you are traveling with a child or someone who requires assistance, secure **your** mask on first, and then assist the other person.*

On the airlines, if you try to be the hero and help everybody else put their mask on in a life-threatening situation and don't put your mask on until the end, you run the risk of running out of air and suffocating.

However, if you secure your mask first, then you are stabilized with that oxygen resource that is very scarce at that altitude, and you could help many more people than you would otherwise be able to without your mask.

It's a similar situation when you work on your personal self. When you are striving towards your personal outcomes, you're more effective with being able to achieve the outcomes that you desire socially and financially. Because you have busted your limiting beliefs and developed a powerful "why," your personal self outcomes will become easier to achieve.

So, what are the outcomes that you can create within this category? They are defined by the following:

Feelings

Fitness

Fun

Feelings encompasses any outcomes that you design to enhance your internal well-being.

For example, you may have feelings outcomes such as:

My outcome is to become a more confident person by communicating with more people.

My outcome is to have a more positive outlook on life and be happier.

My outcome is to spend time each day reviewing a positive motivational message.

Fitness encompasses any outcomes that you design to enhance your physical self.

For example, you may have fitness outcomes such as:

My outcome is to get my body stronger by losing weight.

My outcome is to work out three days per week.

My outcome is to eat better by modifying my diet with healthier food choices.

Fun encompasses any outcomes that you design that bring you more joy and happiness.

For example, you may have fun outcomes such as:

My outcome is to have one weekend a month where I take a fun day trip outside my city.

My outcome is to read an entertaining or inspiring book each month.

My outcome is to treat myself to dinner and a movie.

You can be much more creative with this category and these are but a few examples regarding feelings, fitness, and fun. Feel free to expand upon them as you see fit. The key is this is a template with the understanding that anything that is included within enhancing your life or your internal self is designed to focus on you, creating an enhanced version of yourself.

Your social self

The second of the three main outcomes that you will focus on within the newly delivered and enhanced version of you; the "social" self refers to three powerful entities beyond you, outside of your being. When those are harnessed and appreciated, they will nicely complement the "personal self" you that you are enhancing.

So, what are these three powerful entities?

Your family
Your higher self
Your following

Family doesn't necessarily have to include a significant other or children (especially if you may be single without kids!). Family can represent very close friends, associates, or anyone that you have developed a close or special relationship with. So, try to think outside of the box, understanding that family doesn't have to mean genetic relatives.

Why is it that I feel family is important to enhance? Because our strength lies in our social interactions, having a natural desire to be with others. In the 21st century, this is easily seen by the explosion in social media, with the abundance of options available for people to reach out, many times to strangers! I'm not saying to incorporate your entire list of Facebook friends into your "family." I'm talking about the relationships with deeper bonds.

Regarding family outcomes, you may have some such as:

My outcome is to have weekly and dedicated date nights with my significant other for two months.

My outcome is to spend an extra hour a day in meaningful conversation with my significant other.

My outcome is to visit family members outside of my own home a minimum of two days per month.

Faith is the one that may touch a nerve in some people because of lack of belief in a higher power or some level of skepticism regarding it.

So be it!

It's not to be disrespectful to your beliefs but I understand the power of embracing a higher power and I would suspect that most of the people who read this book do too. Even if you have no belief or skepticism of it, you can consider having the outlook that a higher version of yourself is guiding you along your own path. For me, and many that I have discussed this issue with, there is power in believing that a higher power guides us.

I have seen it in having things unexpectantly turning my way, getting ideas and breakthroughs when most needed, and simply having the pieces of my life fall into place at the right time.

You may call it luck!

If that is what calling it works for you, then go for it!

Some examples of outcomes with faith may include:

My outcome is to read a daily religious passage for 30 days.

My outcome is to attend a spiritual service four times in the next 90 days.

My outcome is to have a daily written journal of gratitude with five things a day I'm grateful for.

Following reflects your impact regarding those around you.

Are you looking to be influential or create and/or enhance the following around you? Meaning, those that you socially interact with?

I believe everyone has value that can be shared with another, no matter how small or insignificant you may feel that it is. You may never know how your words, support, advice, or simple presence can positively influence another, enhancing and benefiting their lives in ways that you simply can't imagine.

Some examples of outcomes that represent your following would be:

My outcome is to post a positive message on Facebook live once per week for four weeks.

My outcome is to do community service in my area for 20 hours over the next 60 days.

My outcome is to send out 20 cards of gratitude to family and friends in the next 90 days.

Again, be creative with the outcomes that you create for your external self.

I can't think of more powerful forces outside of your family and faith that will strengthen your connection with yourself and those who follow you!

Your financial self

The final of the three main outcomes is your financial self. I think of the financial self in various ways:

>**Your internal financial worth**
>
>**Your external financial value**
>
>**Your core financial happiness**

Your **internal financial worth** represents your total income.

Bottom line, any source of income coming in would be encompassed in this.

Some examples of outcomes with your internal financial worth would be:

My outcome is to grow the income in my business by 10% in the next 90 days.

My outcome is to add $5000 to my savings within the next 90 days.

My outcome is to close on five homes in my real estate business in the next 90 days.

Your **external financial value** represents your financial contribution to others, like charities. It doesn't necessarily have to be an actual monetary contribution.

Take the following examples for outcomes regarding your external financial value:

My outcome is to raise $1000 for charity through my garage sale.

My outcome is to spend three days on the team with Habitat for Humanity.

My outcome is to provide free consultative services in my business four hours per month for three months.

Finally, your **core financial happiness** is how you feel about your main source of income. Making a ton of money can be great but the question is, are you happy doing it?

Being in the medical field, burnout among physicians is over 50% and many doctors today go to work just for the paycheck, having lost the passion for it.

Outcomes that you can consider for your core financial happiness would include:

My outcome is to commit four hours per weekend to an occupation or job that I am passionate about.

My outcome is to write down three things that I enjoy about my job and focus on doing them for 30 days.

My outcome is to create a list of three things I do not enjoy about my job and minimize the impact of two of them.

Drafting your different outcomes

After understanding the three types of outcomes, now is the time to draft them out. Don't worry about getting them perfect. You are just writing down outcomes that you feel will serve you.

Take each of the outcome categories, *personal, social,* and *financial,* and write down three outcomes that you would desire for each one, giving you a total of nine outcomes. Again, they don't have to be perfect and feel free to use the previous examples to guide you. Just because they won't be the final version, I still don't want you to rush through them! Take the time to put some thought into them. It's the roadmap towards delivering the enhanced version of yourself, so be patient, put some thought into the process, and come back once you have completed the exercise.

You can download the worksheet for writing down your outcomes at:

https://www.docdeliversbooks.com/free-ebook/

and scroll down to the section called "Develop Your Outcomes."

Welcome back!

By now, you should have your nine outcomes written down. If you don't, stop here and complete the exercise and then come back. Now, you are finishing up your first trimester of growth and development.

As you are completing this section on who you wish to be, I want to reflect upon the amazing growth that you have experienced so far.

I discussed the value of enhancing your core and strengthening your focus in life.

That was followed by getting into the right state of mind for the appropriate upcoming task or situation that you will encounter. Following this, I introduced the concept of future pacing to see your level of success right now, important for seeing your outcome in advance, enhancing your confidence and determination.

I defined the essential difference between goals and outcomes and how you should strive for the latter.

Finally, I discussed, and you created your three main outcomes; your personal, social, and financial selves and how working on all of them will provide you with balance.

Congratulations!

You have just completed your first trimester within the Circle of Conception, so next up is moving into the second trimester. Within you are powerful tools to help move you forward because you are going to need them.

The second trimester transitions from who you wish to "BE" to what you choose to "DO." It's not the main ACTION step in the process, but an important bridge before that step.

There is an entity that cripples most people before even getting to that action step and that is what the second trimester addresses.

What are you going to DO? You will learn to internally DO the things that are essential for overcoming your fears and obstacles holding you back from success.

Chapter 8
Your Second Trimester: DO

Now, you have solidified your understanding of the person that you wish to be. It is very important that you understand this critical point in your transition as you learn what to "do."

This is a point where many people get stuck in life, however I am going to guide you through this pitfall so that you have a much better chance of achieving your goals and outcomes in life and delivering an enhanced version of yourself.

When I talked about the person that you wished to be, I focused on many things, such as your core values and your focus. You were shown the steps that needed to be taken in order to BE the person that you desired but I want you to go beyond that.

I don't want you to BE the person that you desire.

I want you to BECOME the person that you desire.

Now this may sound like it's the exact same thing, but it isn't.

The person that you NEED to BECOME involves you taking internal action. You busted limiting beliefs, developed core values, and instead of just writing them down, now is the time to make them a part of you. For example, you may have had core values of determination, focus and commitment. And yes, you did the things that were necessary in order to create your core values, write them down and reflect upon them. Now, is the time to transition from mentally thinking about your values to doing them daily.

And this is where many people stop because they feel that simply saying or writing down the things that they desire for themselves is enough, but it isn't. The next step that you must take is to transform the person that you wish to be into a person that will **DO** the things that are necessary for overcoming fears and achieving your outcomes.

Let's take a minute to clarify the difference between DO and ACT again.

Both are actions; however, I define them as two succinctly distinct types of actions.

When you **DO**, you are taking *internal action* upon the person that you wanted to **BE**. Taking the *mental actions* necessary to bust your limiting beliefs, develop your core, and soon overcoming your fears.

When you **ACT**, now you are taking *external actions* upon the things that you needed to **DO**. Taking the *physical actions* necessary to overcome your fears and challenges.

Just think of it like this:

When you are "doing," you are taking action towards the person you wish to be internally in the present.

When you are "acting," you are taking action towards the reborn external version of yourself that you desire in the future.

The key questions to ask yourself are:

Do you understand the importance of taking action to enhance yourself?

When you are taking that action every day, no matter how small, does it make sense that you will move closer towards the future version of yourself? Are you moving towards the goals and outcomes that you desire?

The importance of daily action, no matter how small, no matter how challenging it is, no matter how scary it may seem, is the key to success.

And that is why I felt the original definition of *be, do,* and *have* needed to be expanded upon. I felt that the action of DO needed to be refined and separated into a separate internal action. One that is needed to bring out the internal version of yourself now, through your newly busted limiting beliefs and redefined core values.

Despite the challenges and setbacks that you may have experienced before, the second trimester of the Circle of Conception is designed to get you moving forward and deal with the number one thing that holds people back from achieving the goals and outcomes that they desire in life.

For decades, my life was held back in ways I didn't even realize because of one simple thing.

Not being able to swim!

It may sound simple, but it was a debilitating fear that held me back from socializing with others at pool parties, not having fun at the beach, and feeling sad while I saw others swimming in the water with ease and joy.

Once I learned to overcome the fear of swimming, no, let me clarify that, the fear and panic of drowning, it opened up my life to many other adventures in health, spirituality, mental discipline, and just overall fun!

A word with four simple letters—**fear**—has caused millions of lives to come and go from this world unfulfilled, robbing *our* lives of so much untapped knowledge and information. Millions that have taken their ideas and dreams to the grave, not realizing the massive impact that they could have had, not only upon themselves, but the world overall.

It's the reason why I worked long days and nights to grind out the concepts of this book to present it publicly. And if my words can help one person, such as yourself, the effort was well worth it!

Thus, in order to DO and express your internal being, as you continue to flow through this second trimester, you are going to learn to DO the steps that will help you overcome fear.

Doing the thing that is hard

I remember the day like it was yesterday.

Thirty minutes to go before the start of the swim portion of the triathlon.

I was on my third triathlon of the series for the year. This series was brutal for me because it was my transition from swimming in the pool to swimming in open bodies of water. The first two races were disasters, having full-blown panic attacks in the water, and I feared that the biggest one was to come in less than half an hour.

What was I going to do?

I grew up with a lifelong fear of swimming, no let me correct that, a lifelong fear of drowning. I couldn't have fun in the pool, so I had to stay on the sidelines and watch other kids playing in the deep end because I simply would not go down there.

It really wasn't my fault. It started back when I was around eight or nine years old. I remember my father, trying to teach me how to swim by using his methodology of tough love, throwing me into the deep end of the pool. Little did I know how traumatic that event would be for me going forward.

Ever since then, I simply had no desire to get into the pool.

It wasn't fun for me.

It wasn't relaxing.

It just brought up an overwhelming fear of being submerged in the water and not being able to get out.

Two years before that fateful day of my third triathlon swim for the year, I decided that enough was enough and I had to figure out how to conquer my fear of swimming. Step by step, I developed the mindset, hired the coach, and in time, I was able to swim somewhat comfortably in the pool.

However, the open water was a completely different beast.

The first triathlon swim of the year, like I said, was a complete disaster because I suffered a full-blown panic attack. Now as a physician, I understood how debilitating panic attacks could be, but until I was three minutes into my swim, I really didn't appreciate how crippling of an event it could be. I was able to use willpower to complete the swim, but it was not anything that I took any joy in.

The second swim was even worse!

It was a short 600-yard swim, swimming out to the middle of the lake and then making a hairpin turn at 300 yards. Now, about 150 yards into the swim, I was doing okay until I looked up. I noticed that I was drifting off course and was swimming in the direction of those faster swimmers ahead of me that were coming back to shore.

Spinning around in the water, bobbing like a cork with no direction or control, I remember the safety boat coming up to me. I grabbed on the side for dear life, telling myself in my mind that there was no way that I would be able to complete this. The rescue person asked me, "Do you want me to pull you out?" And for a split second that seemed like an eternity, I thought of nothing more than scrambling into the boat, getting back to shore, and just calling it a day.

I didn't understand its significance at that time, but I do understand now. I managed to gain my composure, finish the swim, and complete the triathlon race. It was only the second race and I had a long season ahead of me.

"Twenty minutes to go." That was the overhead announcement going off for all of the racers in this third race of the season.

Little did I know, that day, that moment would be a major turning point in my life. It was a day that I started the process of learning to truly overcome my fear of swimming. I told myself that there were only going to be one of two outcomes with this swim. I was going to swim nonstop without panic, and step out of this lake feeling strong, both mentally and physically. Or, I was going to keep swimming, no matter what fears arose within me, and keep stroking until I literally passed out and the safety patrol would pull my limp body out of the water.

As I was making this declaration to myself and the tears were flowing, a surge of energy rose within me, something that I had not experienced before, and it felt exhilarating. It overwhelmed my senses because I started to lose the sense of fear, the emotion drained out of me and it was replaced with a stronger power…

The power to take action.

"Five minutes to go."

I was in the slowest heat, and there were probably around 200 people in the race, so I would be one of the last to go into the water, having watched several waves ahead of me already start off. I was starting to feel a little embarrassed because I had on one of the colored swim caps, indicating that I was in the slowest heat. I started to tell myself in my mind that this was going to be my day. Without even realizing it or planning this in advance, I started visualizing myself swimming the race, without fear of panic, seeing each stroke, and seeing myself successfully navigate the course without a single break.

I was feeling strong today!

"Thirty seconds to go."

I'm about knee-high in the water and it's feeling cool today but not so cold that it will numb my senses.

For the first time ever before starting a race, I was excited to get started!

I couldn't wait until the announcer said that magical word…

"GO!"

I was off, and I was taking each stroke one by one remembering to stay calm and relaxed. I was slow that day, but I didn't care. It didn't matter that people were passing me because this wasn't about a race or competition with other people.

This was a competition with my mind and fear was not going to win out today!

Three hundred yards in and I started to see the small island in the middle of the lake that was the turning point.

"How the hell did I get here so quickly?!?!?"

I was feeling confident and strong and I unconsciously picked up my pace, not because I wanted to get out of the water quickly but because I knew I still had juice left in the tank and I wasn't going to go home with it today!

"Two hundred yards to go," I told myself, feeling strong and confident.

The people that were passing me in the beginning, those colored caps in my same time group, were starting to go by me and the funny thing was, I was passing them!

Fifty yards to go.

As I was doing my strokes and intermittent sighting to make sure I was still on course and going straight, I could start to more clearly see the people on the shore and hear the cheers of the spectators. Up to this point, my strokes were strong, my breathing was controlled, and I had not panicked.

Not one single time.

The one time that jolted me and caused me to lose my concentration is when my hand scraped a firm surface.

I finally hit land!

I stood up, ran out of the water knowing that my swim was done and as I transitioned to my bike, I took a final look back at the lake that I just conquered, quietly telling myself, "Not today."

This was not to be a day where I panicked.

This was not going to be a day where I dreaded swimming the event.

This was not going to be a day when I couldn't wait to get out of the water.

This was going to be the day when I decided to take that first step and take back control of the power that I knew I had within me.

That was a fantastic day!

CHAPTER 9
F.E.A.R. (AND THE THINGS YOU DO TO GET PAST IT)

I tell the story because it was a turning point in my life where I acted against fear, and in time, slowly learned how to overcome and control it. It wasn't a process that happened overnight but as I look back on that experience and the many triathlon races after that, I slowly began to recognize and discover the small steps, the small shifts, that helped me get from the point of having full-blown panic attacks in the water to having fun during my swims.

The confidence that I gained from swimming has spilled over to so many other aspects of my life. It has strengthened me mentally, allowing me to be more successful in other areas of my life. It has enhanced my relationship with family, friends, and loved ones. It has helped me create a mindset of a much healthier lifestyle. It has enhanced my ability to engage in business opportunities without fear, helping generate financial abundance on a level that I did not think was possible.

I learned that I was not alone, and I knew that many people had fears of swimming. What I didn't realize was how fear can keep people from achieving the outcomes that they desire in life. Even worse, it prevented them from even starting things that they wished to achieve.

In my process of evaluating my fear, I systemized the necessary steps to act against it. As time went on, I realized that I had a powerful process that needed to be shared with other people. It was wonderful to be able to conquer this challenge but what is even more empowering is showing, teaching, and guiding others to do the exact same thing.

I think about those early childhood years watching my friends and family and loved ones play in the water and having fun in the pool. It was painful recalling that I missed out on those childhood opportunities because I let fear cripple me and dictate the terms of my living.

Childhood is such a magical and fun time in our lives. Remembering the things that I lost out on helped drive me to write this book. It's fulfilling and rewarding to help other people not miss out on the things that they truly want and desire to do in their own lives.

There are a series of questions that I want you to ask yourself:

"What have I lost out on in my life because of fear?"

"Am I open to looking at my fear in a different way?"

"Am I ready to DO the necessary steps to start to challenge and overcome my fear?"

These questions focus on how fear has affected your past and present.

Hopefully they gave you some perspective on how fear has held you back from achieving the goals and outcomes that you desire. Everyone has fears, whether they see them or not, acknowledge them or not. The great thing is that you can take a systemized approach towards overcoming them.

Ask yourself these powerful questions, and as you read them and formulate the answers, you will begin to realize that fear is only a tiny spec of your total being.

"Do you fear everything?"

Likely, probably not.

Some of things that you probably do not fear could be things such as eating, walking, or going into your home.

You probably don't have a significant fear of going to sleep or using the bathroom throughout the day.

Why?

Because these are things in your life that you do automatically and take for granted, and that is the mindset that we're going to develop within you with regards to the way that you visualize fear.

I remember growing up in New York City and when I hit 18 years old I was excited about getting my learner's permit. Now I could have done it a year or two earlier. However, if you've ever driven in New York City, that is an adventure that can put fear in even the most experienced drivers.

I don't think I've ever experienced a city with drivers that have the lethal combination of driving fast and reckless at the same time. However, after experiencing my first year in college and seeing the fellas on the campus driving around in their own cars, I decided to take the plunge and get my learner's permit.

Getting on the Brooklyn Queens Expressway (the "BQE" for my fellow Brooklynites) the first time was nothing short of a life altering experience. Now, if you haven't had the pleasure of driving on this expressway, it is fast, tight, and can be intimidating. I remember the first time I drove on the expressway. With my dad sitting beside me, he guided me towards the middle lane so other cars could easily go around me.

My dad was encouraging me to speed up so that we would not get rear-ended by other cars. I looked down at the speedometer and even though I felt I was driving really fast I was only going a mere 45 mph.

Way too slow for the BQE, and a recipe for disaster!

After a couple of months, driving on this highway was just second nature. And in time, instead of having a fear of driving on this highway, I started to have fun and looked forward to the drives.

Today, driving on highways is second nature and many times, as you probably experienced it, you just drive unconsciously, miles going by, and not even realizing the journey that you are taking.

I say this because there are many things that you take for granted today that are second nature to you. They are things that you feared doing the first time. However, as time progressed, and you did the thing more, you began to chip away at the fear, diminishing its power upon you. You have proven to yourself that you have overcome fear in the past. Because of this, you can overcome any fears that you have now. You have done it before and you will do it again!

What are the reasons we fear things in our lives?

Some of the more common reasons why people have fears would be:

1. Fear of failure. Not living up to others' expectations.

2. Worry about criticism or negative feedback.

3. Unable to see the immediate benefits.

4. Not able to see or accept the outcome.

5. The task or event appears too complex.

6. Feeling overwhelmed with the amount of challenges that are presented. The task or challenge not being congruent with your core values.

To summarize it, fear is broken down into the mnemonic of P.A.N.I.C.

Preoccupied – with the worry of failing or with the fear itself, which can cause a vicious cyclical loop of fearing the actual fear.

Absent – not having the skills or proper values or knowledge to achieve your outcome.

No – having no experience if the outcome has not been attempted in the past.

Intense expectations – that are put on by ourselves or put on us by others, because there is a sense of being overwhelmed or overreaching beyond what we, or others, think we can do.

Critical – being critical of ourselves and having self-doubt or pity

Reflect upon an outcome that you desired in your life that you have yet to achieve. Three of the more common excuses that people make with regards to not achieving the outcomes that they desire are related to time, finances, and self-understanding.

All of these are tied into fear on some level. Think about it.

If you make the excuse that you do not have enough time to go for your dreams and desires, is time really the issue or is there an underlying fear that is allowing you to use time as an excuse?

When you say that you don't have the finances to go for your goals, is the lack of money truly the issue or is there the fear of losing what you have right now? Or perhaps it's a fear of reaching out and facing rejection while trying to get the funds that you desire.

If you don't understand the path towards getting your goals, do you really not understand where to start? Is it possible that you do understand it slightly but fear it will be too mentally challenging in the long run? So right now, think about two or three reasons why you haven't achieved the outcome that you desire. When you look very closely at those three reasons, is there an underlying fear that you truly haven't seen before?

"As I start to overcome my fear, how would life begin to look for me?"

This is the fun part because you get to brainstorm and create the reality that you desire, where fear is not an option. We're not at the point that we are fully learning to SEE (that's the next trimester!), we are simply imagining how life can possibly look if fear was not an option.

Let's reflect back to the 18-year-old me that was first learning how to drive, imagining how life looked when fear was removed from the picture. I would possibly see myself as the guy that's driving around town picking up his friends, going on dates, and feeling like that powerful and bad-ass teenager that is taking life by the horns! I could see myself driving around campus, having fun on the weekends, not having to rely on the bus or walking home late at night.

So, using an example that you have written, if fear was removed from the equation and you achieve that specific goal and outcome, how would life look for you?

Ask yourself these additional questions:

Are you having more fun and happiness?

Are you achieving plans and goals that are making your life more balanced and fulfilled?

How are you feeling emotionally about yourself? Are the people that are around you responding differently because you've achieved what you desired?

To download the worksheets for this section, simply go to:

https://www.docdeliversbooks.com/free-ebook/

and scroll down to the section called "Understanding Your Fears."

As you answer these questions and reflect upon them, you will begin to look at and feel your fears in a unique way. Not from a negative aspect but from the perspective of someone who has the capability of achieving any and all things they desire and deserve.

The evolution of fear

One of the main reasons why man was able to survive and evolve over thousands of years was because of the development of our innate and automatic response system which is commonly known as "fight or flight."

This was first discovered and recognized by Walter Cannon, an American physiologist of Harvard University. He first presented his findings and theories in his book, "The Wisdom of the Body," published in 1932.

Without going into the technical details of physiology, with a focus more on the overall concept of the response, it was essential for protecting our early ancestors. In simplistic terms, the fight or flight response enhances a multitude of stress hormones within our physiology, which can cause a physical body response that can include several factors:

Dilating the pupils and enhancing your visual acuity.

Increasing your heart rate and blood pressure as well as your breath rate.

Enhancing your mental focus, awareness and alertness.

Decreasing your perception of discomfort and pain.

Diminished blood flow to the frontal cortex of the brain which can control logical and rational thought and actions.

So why would this be important in our early human development?

Think about it. When we were in our evolutionary stage, we had to rely on *hunting* game for our basic needs, while at the same time being the *hunted*.

When we were threatened by animals that could seriously maim or kill us, we had to have a response that was built in; an automatic order to enhance our survival. Thus, an event which caused us stress, fear, or worry, would automatically trigger this response system, essentially putting us in a heightened state and protective mode.

At the time, this was necessary for survival, and understand this, it is still very necessary today. However, the number of stimuli that trigger this response is multiplied on a massive magnitude.

These days, we don't have to worry about any significant random attacks of large animals as we casually walk down the street, however, there are many other stressors that can still trigger the fight or flight response.

What are some of them?

Feeling overwhelmed at work.

Getting stressed out with upcoming projects or deadlines in the workplace.

Feeling stressed with our finances.

Getting overwhelmed with our duties at home or family responsibilities.

These are just a few of the many things that we are imparted with daily that can trigger the fight or flight response system. No wonder why we are potentially in a constant state of stress. There are so many more triggers in the 21st century that will cause the massive dump of stress hormones in our system which put us in that state. Now, there is nothing that we can do about the automatic response that is built within our system. In fact, it is there for our protection and we do need and require it because there are legitimate events that can happen in our lives which need to trigger the response.

What if you needed to get out of a burning building to save yourself and your family?

What if you needed to help a victim escape from a car crash or save a drowning man?

This automated response, which is driven by your subconscious and that you are not able to hormonally control, does have its benefits.

However, the self-triggered mechanisms are ones which you can absolutely control. They are not automated like your fight or flight response system. These are events that are built and driven by your conscious system.

By using the right strategies and techniques, you can overcome the fear which triggers the fight or flight response.

Misconceptions of fear

The question to ask yourself is that when you think of fear, do you have a predefined conception of what fear represents?

Here are some of the more common misconceptions of fear:

Being a fearful person means that you were weak and unworthy.

No one can relate to or understand the fear that I'm going through.

When you are fearful that simply means that you lack the confidence to do what you need to do.

There is no need to even try because I will never get rid of the fear 100%.

Because you are fearful that means that you have done something wrong.

Having a fear is a sign that you were not meant to even do that task in the first place.

You must have courage to start with to conquer the fear in the first place.

This is probably the biggest misconception with regards to fear because many people have the mindset that you must have a certain level of discipline, courage, or strength to overcome the fear in the first place. Understand this, that these are "emotions" but an essential piece to overcome the fear has nothing to do with emotion.

It has to do with taking action.

When I was sitting in my car 20 minutes before starting the swimming leg of the race, I had a powerful revelation. Despite still having the fear,

I knew what had to be done that day. It was not my **emotional state** that helped me overcome the fear that day. It was my mindset and internal **action state** that drove me to swim the race

Where does our fear develop?

When our fear develops, it is typically associated with an event that can either be mental, emotional, spiritual, or physical. That event triggers a set point, let's say an anchor, which is a foundation for anything that is related to the fear going forward.

Let's take the example of an adult who has a fear of dogs. I can relate to this because I saw this exactly with my mother. As far as I've known, my mom has had a lifelong fear of dogs and I don't know what the traumatic event was. You probably heard the stories of children that have been bitten by dogs in early childhood and as grown adults, they carry that fear with them. They have the same level of fear they had as a child.

Essentially, what they have done is create an association of dogs with pain. So, when this adult sees a dog, it triggers the fight or flight response because they are subconsciously putting themselves into a protection mode to avoid any potential injury from the dog. The fight or flight mode eliminates the rational thought they would normally have where they could consciously think and assess the situation. They can't see that this dog may not have any ill intentions whatsoever and simply wants to be friendly. That's because of the association that was created many years ago.

So, the fear created an association, where any similar event that is related to the original fear triggers the fight or flight response. They are like anchors that drag us down.

These anchors can be developed in childhood events. It's like the anchor that I created for myself with a lifelong fear of swimming because my fear of getting in the water triggered the response that I would go under and struggle to get back to the surface. Anchors can also be created with other situations such as:

Having a **previous failure** in life with a task or event that you did not complete. For example, this could be a failure in an interview to get a specific job. Because of that previous failure, you developed fear to the point that you avoid the attempt to take the interview again, panic during the taking of other ones, having thoughts of the previous failure.

Verbal input from other people that embeds within our subconscious. For example, we may be told that "we are worthless" or that "we will never amount to anything in life." When these anchors are created by the verbal actions of authoritative figures, such as parents, teachers, or coaches, it can have a detrimental effect going forward.

Visualization input by witnessing other people experience a negative outcome in their own goals. When combined with a lower self-esteem, they develop the mindset that, "If that person can't complete the tasks there's no way that I will be able to do it." For example, you may witness a close friend or colleague fail in a startup business venture, which creates an anchor in your mindset that attempts made by you will result in the same failure.

Physical input, as described with the example of being bitten by the dog in early childhood, creates the anchor where the fight or flight response is triggered to put you in a protection mode from future pain.

How is it represented?

When we are in a state of fear, it can be represented by several physiological responses which can be visualized by ourselves or other people externally or felt by ourselves internally. They are broken down into our senses, the three main ones which are visual, auditory, and kinesthetic—also known as our physical feelings. Fear can also be represented in the other two senses; smell and taste, however they are less prominent than the main three that were initially described.

Visually, we may experience a loss of focus or the reverse, we may experience heightened focus.

Auditory, it can be a ringing in the ears or having a complete loss of the surrounding sounds.

Kinesthetically, it can be represented as sweating, increased heart rate, shortness of breath, or physical weakness.

It's important to bring these up now because as you go more into the techniques of overcoming fear, you must understand the physical manifestations of it. Once you recognize them, it's easier to learn how to overcome them.

With an understanding of how fear works and how it manifests, let's take the necessary steps to work on getting past it.

Redefining F.E.A.R.

Before we start this journey on helping you to identify, discover, and conquer your fear, you need to start with the basic understanding of it, looking at each of the components that it encompasses.

You probably heard fear defined as "false evidence appearing real" or some people take the more comical approach and say, "forget everything and run." However, this is an entirely serious matter that affects millions of people's lives in a very negative way. Thus, the important step you need to internally DO is face and overcome your fears.

I'm going to redefine the traditional definition of fear. Through my research, study, and coaching I have created a much more powerful mnemonic that will serve you much better.

The way that I define fear is as a process that will help you flow more effectively through your life. You will take the necessary steps to start conquering the fear and then reinforce this pattern in the cyclical loop, continuing to stack upon the foundation that is built.

The way that I define fear is with the following mnemonic:

F – "FOCUS"

E – "ENHANCE"

A – "ACCEPT AND ACT"

R – "RECALL, REASSESS and REENGAGE"

Overcoming fear is a never-ending loop. You evaluate it, enhance your mindset as you DO the steps to overcome it, take physical action, evaluate your progress, and repeat the process. As you continue to cycle, you take more action, overcome more of the fear, and it becomes an automatic process for you.

Let's take a visual look at this concept:

As the chapter progresses, I will present each specific component in much more detail. So far, as you have been reading and listening to my story and seeing how I overcame fear, you will begin to realize that the process to overcoming fear can be broken down into simple steps that will greatly enhance your ability to overcome your own fears.

F.E.A.R. (Understanding FOCUS)

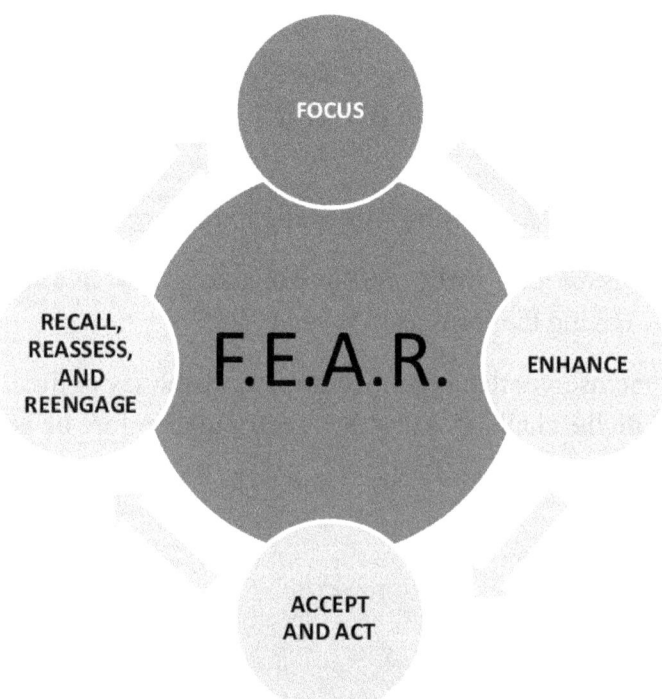

Having you focus on the right things is the first of the four steps that are necessary in overcoming your fears.

Focus on your state (step 1 of FOCUS)

Being in the right state is important for overcoming your fears. Let's reflect again upon the simplified model of be, do and have:

The correct model for everyday life

Now, under normal circumstances, this is absolutely the way that tasks, challenges, or desired dreams and outcomes should be approached. Normally, you will want to start with having the mindset that is necessary such as being confident or happy or powerful because that's going to drive the events that you wish to do so that you can have the outcome that you seek.

In this model you are starting with *an emotional state.*

Here's the issue that many people run into. They live their life in reverse by having the formula in reverse.

They tell themselves that once they **have** more money or time, they will be able to **do** the challenges that they seek and therefore **be** happier and fulfilled:

The incorrect model for everyday life

Now, the reason why this is incorrect is because you are starting with a **thing.**

You are starting with something in a **physical state** (or non-emotional items) as the driving force that's going to get you into the emotional state that you desire. The problem with this way of thinking is that you haven't built the ***emotional state*** that is critical in achieving your desired outcome. You are striving to have what you desire without developing the emotional state needed to support it.

You must make a slight tweak in that model when dealing with fear and here's the reason why:

When dealing with fear, people fall into the trap of feeling that they must be confident **before they take any action.** But in this case, the action must be taken **first** in order to develop the confidence over time.

So instead of focusing on the *emotional state,* such as motivation or confidence, we're going to focus on **an action state**.

Now, this is your modified flow of have, do and be when you are taking the necessary steps to overcome fear:

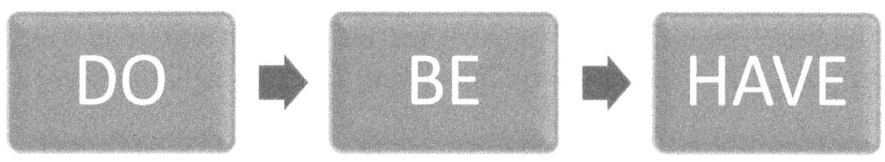

The correct model for overcoming fear

Instead of having a mindset of "I choose to be motivated" you have the mindset of "I choose to move forward with action."

Why is it that we do it this way?

The reason is you are trying to minimize the effects of the fight or flight response. That is triggered when you are in an emotional state and because it is an automatic response, it can be quite challenging to overcome. However, instead of overwhelming yourself with emotion, you overwhelm yourself with taking action first. By doing this, you can make the attempt to try to bypass this automatic trigger response before it has its full effect.

Going back to my example of overcoming the fear of swimming and drowning, I took the mental action first of deciding that I was going to swim no matter what emotional state I was in. My action was my priority and my driving force for starting the swim that day. I still did have some underlying fear, but that was overridden by a strong action that I committed to that day.

And in each subsequent race, by continuing to focus on taking action first, **then** I started building the confidence, and having more confidence in the event equaled and exceeded the level of the action that I initially started with.

It's a powerful tool in a completely different way of thinking!

"Am I open to looking at my fear in a different way?"

This is you stepping outside of the box!

And when you accept and acknowledge this different way of thinking, the possibilities for you overcoming your fears are going to become much easier. As you take more action, you build more confidence which leads back to you taking even more action. Once the process begins, each action step to overcome your fear becomes less challenging.

Using your core values to overcome fear (step two of FOCUS)

Have you ever eaten an avocado?

I love them because they give me an essential boost of the healthy fats that I need in my diet, especially given my triathlon training.

But that is not the reason why I bring that up today. When you look at various trees that can bear fruit, they are all special, but what I love about the avocado tree is that it has its quick spurt of fast growth and longer time for maturation. If you take the pit of an avocado, stick three or four toothpicks in it, fill up a glass of water and then suspend the pit on the edge of the glass so that the bottom half of the pit is in contact with the water, you'll be able to see the roots emerge from the bottom of the pit in a few weeks, usually around four to six.

The next phase of this rapid growth cycle is that you're going to start to see one or more shoots start to emerge from the top of the pit and once this happens, you start to see the pit crack and split open. Once this occurs, it's time to put this delicate and growing seed within a pot with nutrient rich soil and warm water.

In time, in about five years sometimes upwards of 15, your young avocado tree will start to bear fruit of its own. The key is to maintain it in a healthy and warm environment with plenty of sun, water, nourishment, and loving care.

When I talk about your life, there is a core within your being that is tough, resilient, and if nurtured in the right way like the avocado pit, will grow and blossom soon to produce the fruits of your own labor. It will take time because it's a delicate process to develop yourself. However, if you use the right ingredients and take care to evaluate and reassess the steps along the process, you too will be able to develop the strong core that is needed for your foundation to overcome the fears within your own life.

Think of real-life like that of the avocado.

When you are living a life of fear, your exterior is tough, resistant, and resilient because your fear envelops you like the tough skin of the avocado. There is no nutritional value in the skin of the avocado like there is no value in having your core enveloped with fears.

Beneath this thin skin of the avocado is the soft, edible, nourishing part. The avocado is rich in unsaturated fats which are the optimal ones to have in our diet. On the other hand, we have fats in our diet such as trans or saturated fats that are not good for us. It is the same way in our lives where we may have dreams, desires and outcomes that are healthy for us or may not be so healthy for us.

And finally, we have the most important portion of the avocado which is the inner core. It's that rock-hard seed that when tended to properly, replanted, and nourished will grow and bear the next generation of avocados to continue the process.

The core of the avocado is not much different than the core values that you have for yourself. The core values are the concepts and beliefs within your life that guide you towards the person that you wish to be.

These could be values like honor, focus, commitment, or any number of hundreds of different values that could resonate with you.

If you don't understand what your core values are, then how can you **grow into** the outcomes and desires that you choose in life?

If your life is enveloped in a hard exterior of fear, then how will you be able to **get past** that fear to achieve the outcomes and desires that you wish in life?

So, there is a lesson that I need to share with you that goes beyond simply showing you the strategy and techniques for overcoming your fear to get to the life that you desire. We must also work at not just stating but *living* your core values. Without them, it's more challenging to overcome the fear and get your desired goals and outcomes. Having strong core values will reinforce the actions you take to overcome your fears. Good thing you developed them in your first trimester!

Life is a process where you are constantly evolving and constantly maturing. You evolve as you start living based off your core values. Once you have a set of core values that you follow, it builds the platform for helping you overcome the fears that you have in your life. And once you break through these fears, you will begin to achieve the goals and outcomes that you desire.

They're going to provide the inspiration, not only to yourself, but also for those that are around you.

Ask yourself this question:

Do you feel more inspired by the person who is confident and always looking to help other people or do you feel more inspired by the person who is selfish and always putting people down?

Your core values are your maps of life. They provide the guidance that you will need to continue moving towards outcomes that you desire. You will stay on a pathway that is essential to help you overcome the fears that hold you back from those outcomes in the first place.

Now that you have the right focus on your fears, it's time to enhance the things that will help you overcome them.

F.E.A.R. (Enhancing you)

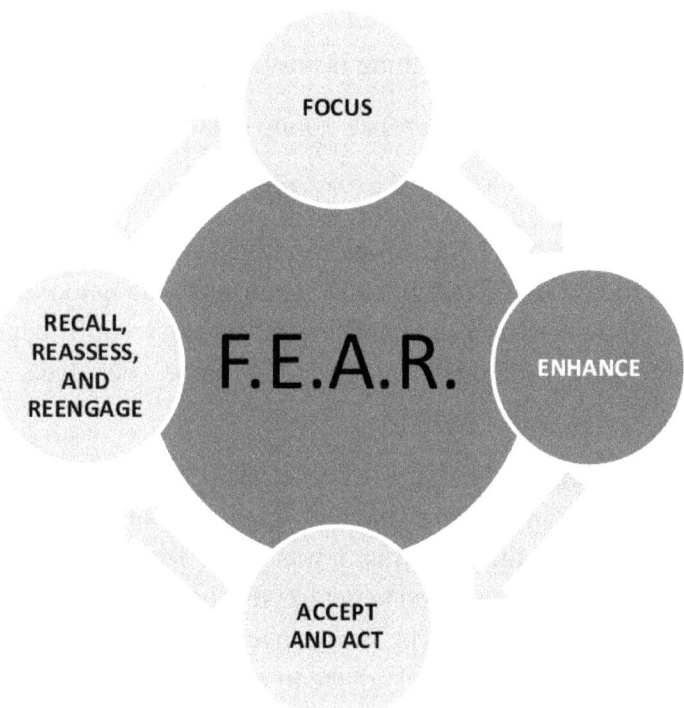

Enhancing your thoughts is the next step in overcoming fear. You will do this by enhancing your language, the way you look at fear, how you physically respond to it, and looking at success in a new way.

Let's start with elevating your language.

Enhancing Your Language to Overcome Fear

"How you do anything is how you do everything."

This was a success quote by the motivational speaker T. Harv Eker, but when applied to the mental mindset that we wish to develop, a quote that we should utilize is:

> "How we think about anything is how we act about everything."
>
> – Terence Young MD

Many years ago, when I was a junior in high school, I remember being brought to the office of my guidance counselor, the name escapes me to this day, however as you hear more of the story you'll begin to see the reason why I decided to erase her name, her face, and her "experience" out of my memory.

So, when I was brought into the office of, shall we say, Ms. Brown, she asked me about my plans beyond high school. And being the authoritative figure that she was, I was eager for her to listen to my overall plans and I was excited to get her feedback and expertise. Being only age 16 at the time and Ms. Brown over 40, I felt that she would be able to provide me with useful advice to help me along with my plans.

This thought process couldn't have been further from the truth.

Now, a little bit of the back story is that I grew up with a lifelong desire to serve people and my way of achieving this was to become a doctor. As far back as I can remember, I wanted to help people. I remember as a child walking around the house with a pen, thinking it was a medication to give someone. I would stick them and say, "I'm going to fix you with my medicine now."

The obvious next step in the process was to continue to college, get into medical school, and then finally fulfill my lifelong dream of becoming a physician.

However, on this day Ms. Brown had, shall we say, "alternate plans" for the career path that I should pursue. I remember telling her, "Ms. Brown, I'm looking to go on to Morehouse College and from there, on to medical school. I have always wanted to be a doctor."

The reply that I received from her shocked me.

Basically, she told me that I should focus on going to a trade school because she did not feel that I had the grades or tenacity to be able to make it in college, let alone medical school. She crapped all over my dreams and for a few months after that, I had the mindset that I in fact may not be good enough to become a physician.

I fed into her reality and had the mindset that becoming a physician may not be realistic at this time. So, I started looking at alternate occupations that were "easier and not as challenging." Without even realizing it, I questioned if I had what it took to be a doctor. I was a step away from giving up that dream as I started to believe that I was not good enough.

However, in time, I developed the mindset that I would achieve my dream of becoming a doctor no matter what. But in order to develop it, I really had to change my internal communication with myself.

The reason why I bring this story to light is to show you that it is very important to enhance your language, bringing it to a point that works in your favor.

"How do you communicate with yourself?"

Does the way that you talk to yourself uplift you? Does it bring feelings of positivity? Or is it the type of language that creates an atmosphere of self-doubt, or negativity?

"How do others communicate with you?"

Does the communication that others have with you elevate and encourage you? Or is it the type of language that brings you down or diminishes your self-worth?

The communication that we have with ourselves and with others can move our lives in productive and nonproductive ways.

The communication with others can be controlled to an extent. Meaning, if you talk with people that bring you down, simply walk away or let them know not to use that language. What people tell you externally does not have to become your reality. Have the mindset that only accepts thoughts or comments that move you forward in productive ways. The communication that we have with ourselves internally is the more challenging one to control. It's not as easy to walk away from yourself but it can be done! Like talking to someone else, your internal communication does not have to become your reality. The key is to be mindful of having positive language. It's not your job nor is it realistic to have positive thoughts 100% of the time. However, it is possible to have positive thoughts more often than not. Once you do this, overcoming your fears and challenges will become easier as time progresses.

Here are some of the list of the things that we may tell ourselves, particularly when we are approaching an event or outcome or situation that causes us to be afraid:

"It's too hard."

"I'm too scared to do it."

"I'm worried about the future results or worried about failing in the future."

"I don't have the skills to even take the challenge on in the first place."

"Others say that it is impossible and very difficult to do."

"I don't have the money to be able to do what I like to do."

"I don't have the time in my life right now to do what I want to do."

"I don't even know where to start."

Do you see how this relates to our previous definition of having thoughts of P.A.N.I.C.?

Preoccupied – with the worry of failing or preoccupied with the fear itself which can cause a vicious cyclical loop of fearing the actual fear.

Absent – not having the skills or proper values or knowledge to achieve your outcome.

No – having no experience if the outcome has not been attempted in the past.

Intense expectations – that are put on us by ourselves or others because there is a sense of being overwhelmed or overreaching beyond what we or others think we can do.

Critical – being critical of ourselves and having self-doubt or pity.

So, the next step is to enhance your internal language by having thoughts that are C.A.L.M.I.N.G.

Enhancing your thoughts to overcome fear

As you further enhance your internal language consciously, you begin to enhance it subconsciously. As anything that we do new in life that we're not used to, it will take time. It's not a process that will happen overnight because it is repetitive practice that will get you there. Talking to yourself in a positive way every day will help you develop the mindset to overcome your fears.

I created the mnemonic for C.A.L.M.I.N.G. thoughts because I wanted to provide an easy way (not just for me but for the people that I know that I would eventually be coaching in the future) to remember the power statements that I am feeding to my subconscious.

So, when I am thinking of **C.A.L.M.I.N.G.** thoughts, here are the power statements that I personally use:

"I'm **C**onfident that I can...."

"I take **A**ction today to get closer to the outcomes tomorrow."

"**L**ife becomes more exciting as I grow out of my fear."

"**M**emories of success are within me."

"**I** can do anything for…"

"**N**ow is the time to act."

"**G**rowth is what I strive for, each and every day."

Notice that the statements, "I take action today to get closer to the outcomes tomorrow," and "Now is the time to act," both say to act. The reason why I included two of these action statements is because action is one of your more critical steps to overcome your fear, so I felt the need to reinforce its importance.

The fifth statement, which is, "I can do anything for…" and the first statement "I'm confident that I can do …" are generalized statements that I left open to allow you flexibility. When I personally use them, I see myself utilizing them a lot during my triathlon training workouts.

There are sometimes when I'm in the middle of a multiple-hour bike ride or run and I feel like I am mentally and physically burning out and can't complete the task at hand. This would be an example when I insert my statement "I can do anything for…"

What I've found effective for me is that I take the remainder of the task at hand and break it into manageable pieces. For example, if I have two hours left on a bike ride, I may tell myself that, "I can do anything for 10 more minutes." I'm setting myself up with many targets to allow me to focus more on the next waypoint, instead of getting overwhelmed with fear or panic over the overall goal. It is much easier to absorb and digest having the strength to do that activity for 10 minutes instead of thinking of it as a two-hour finale.

That is the reason why the process of overcoming fear is not a linear path. It is a series of taking multiple steps over and over to gradually breakdown the process. So, when you can focus on smaller waypoints or mini outcomes, you can start to develop that confidence as each one is achieved and continue to build smaller levels of confidence that will eventually compound over time.

Again, many times we may find that we *panic* in our language, but it is essential to have *calming* thoughts in order to have the mindset that is optimal for overcoming fear.

Enhance the way you visualize fear

One of the more critical things to do when you're having fearful thoughts is to identify and acknowledge them. You want to recognize then acknowledge the fact that you are having fearful thoughts because once acknowledged, you will take the necessary steps to push them away.

It can be very challenging to eliminate the fear 100%. You don't want to because fear does have a power that you can harness later to your benefit.

What you do want to do is acknowledge that it is there and recognize it for what it is, a mental or verbal P.A.N.I.C. excuse that you use upon yourself.

Begin by acknowledging that you are having that fearful thought. Bring it out into the open so that you can begin to diminish its power and hold over you.

So how do we acknowledge that it is present?

There are several ways that you can do this, such as:

Creating an **auditory response** recognizing that it is here.

Some examples of this could be saying, "My fear is sneaking up on me," or "Mr. Fear is trying to sneak back in."

Creating a **visual statement** or response that causes a pattern interrupt, causing you to break the emotional state of the fear.

Some examples of this could be visualizing the fear within a balloon that blows up and dissipates or seeing the fear written into the soft sand of an ocean beach that is washed away with the waves.

Finally, you can create a **kinesthetic statement or physical response** that will take your mind off the fear and break its emotional state.

Some examples of doing this could be creating a physical anchor point such as tapping your temple, snapping your fingers, or putting your hand over your heart.

The purpose of all these things is that you want to use your visual, auditory, or kinesthetic senses and acknowledge the fear so that you learn how to eventually accept its presence and acknowledge that it is there. Once you do that then you can go on to the next step, which is the transition from having a mindset of P.A.N.I.C. to one of C.A.L.M.I.N.G.

So, for example, say that you have an extreme fear of flying. I was afraid of flying many years ago and I was able to overcome it using these very strategies. The funny thing was I had no name for them at the time!

When I had my fear of flying, I would get nervous when there were any bumps. It was so bad that even with the slightest turbulence, I would have the fear that it was way worse. It was a fear of an event that wasn't even happening.

The process that you would use in this example would be to first verify P.A.N.I.C. by telling yourself something such as, "This fear of flying thing is coming back right now," or you can visualize turbulent colored air within a clear balloon that eventually pops and dissipates away or finally you could snap your fingers and tell yourself, "This fear of flying thing is coming back right now."

There's no right answer to doing this and I included all the various senses because depending on your dominant sensory personality, I wanted to be able to provide you with the necessary variations that resonate best with you.

After acknowledging the fear is there, you would then state your C.A.L.M.I.N.G. thoughts.

I would utilize one of my power statements such as, "I'm confident I can fly in his plane for five more minutes." This sets you up for having a victory over the fear. Once you have one victory, each subsequent one helps make the fear less overall for you. And it doesn't have to be one statement, it can be a multitude of statements that you use for yourself. You can stack this with another statement such as, "I will slowly conquer my fear of flying today so that I can be more confident tomorrow."

Remember, the C.A.L.M.I.N.G. statements are there just as a guideline for you, so you can modify and tweak them in any way that you feel fit or feel that best resonates with you.

These first two steps, verify and verbalize, are very powerful. The key to this trifecta of how you look at fear is in the power of imagination.

Visualization is a very powerful technique for tapping into your subconscious and overcoming fear.

When we are born, there are essentially only two fears that are built into our subconscious, which are the fear of loud noises and the fear of falling.

Every other fear that we generate to our lives is a fear that *we* have created within our own subconscious.

Thus, if we can train our subconscious to have a newly created fear, then at the same time we could also train our subconscious to overcome it through visualization.

Remember one definition of FEAR, false evidence appearing real? If we go with the premise that our fears are nothing more than false manifestations that we have created within our mind, then we can do the opposite and create manifestations that overcome the fear within our mind.

Basically, what I am saying is that if we have the mindset that we have a fear of flying then we can create the visualization within our mind of the opposite.

So, I'm back to our example of flying on the plane. If we are starting to experience some unsettling bumps that causes the fear levels to rise, the next step would be to simply close your eyes and visualize ourselves being calm and relaxed during the flight and having minimal to no thoughts or sensations of fear.

Now obviously, this would be optimal to practice before the fear even comes on in the first place, but it can be used in this situation.

Ideally, you would want to use the steps of ***verifying panic, verbalize calming,*** **and** ***visualizing success*** before you take on the task that causes you the fear and anxiety, but it can be used in a pinch during the event of the fear itself.

I made it more realistic by visualizing the plane starting to be a little bumpy and things starting to get a little rougher. I would see myself having minimal fear during this turbulence and that it eventually went away, continuing with an uneventful flight and finally landing and watching myself walk off the plane.

Understand that the subconscious does not know the difference between reality and fantasy so why not use that to your advantage?

If your subconscious doesn't know that the visual picture that you are creating within your mind is one of thought and not actual reality, then why would you not want to use this to your advantage?

Therefore, I recommend using the visualization technique upon your fear for five to 10 minutes every day.

Get into the habit of practicing visualization in advance. When you encounter the event that causes you to be afraid, then you are more empowered to take advantage of all three steps that are within this process. Once the fear comes on, you can verify the fears, verify the panic, proceed with your calming statement, and then finally topping it off with running the preformed visual movie within your mind that shows you overcoming the fear and having success.

Now how can we make your visualization even more powerful?

The way to make this powerful is to make your visualization as authentic and detailed as possible. Detailed like you are watching a 3D IMAX film where all the sights and sounds are enhanced. What do I mean by this?

You want to be able to see everything that is around you, as far as the colors, textures, the shapes and sizes, and everything else to a very minute detail.

You want audio playing in the background like a surround sound system where you may hear yourself talking to yourself or you hear other people around you, obviously stating positive intentions and thoughts, while incorporating realistic sounds around you.

You want to be able to describe what you are feeling at this point, such as the temperature of the environment in which you are within and how it feels to you or any breezes or sensations that you feel against your skin.

You want to be able to describe the smells that are in the environment.

You want to describe any things that you may be eating or tasting at the time. Imagine the sensations you get from your taste buds.

Utilize all five of your senses to create the most realistic and powerful visualization possible because the more realistic it is the more powerful and more accepting your subconscious is going to be and take hold of it.

Now, if you don't think this is very powerful, let me give you an example of visualization at its finest!

There's an athlete in history that has 28 Olympic medals, of which 23 are gold. In the 2008 Olympic Games in Beijing, he broke a 26-year-old record of seven first-place finishes at any single Olympic Games by capturing eight gold medals. If you don't know who this most decorated and successful Olympian of all time is, let me tell you that we are describing the one and only:

Michael Phelps.

Many people like to focus on the physical attributes of Michael Phelps because he has the perfect physique for being such a phenomenal swimmer. Standing at 6'4", he has multiple physical attributes which make him ideal for swimming such as:

His significant arm span allows him to gain much more distance in the pool than the average swimmer with each stroke.

His relatively shorter legs, given his height, help reduce the drag in the pool and increases speed.

His above average lung capacity allows him to have a higher level of endurance in the water.

His double-jointed ankles and arms allow him to generate more power in the water.

His upper body strength that is generated from his unusually long torso, which is disproportionate to his given height.

While his physical attributes may be the envy of other elite swimmers, there is one unseen factor that cannot be measured and is invisible to the naked eye.

It's his mental mindset and powerful visualization techniques.

Michael Phelps has utilized visualization techniques from an early age that were taught to him by his swim coach and sports psychologist Bob Bowman.

In order to help Michael Phelps with his mental training, he taught him powerful visualization techniques that would have him visualize his races from so many different perspectives.

As Bob Bowman described it, Michael Phelps would visualize the races from a **localized perspective** where he would visualize himself from the start of the blocks, swimming during the race, finishing the race in victory, and seeing his own celebration and success. He also stated that Phelps would also see the race from a more **global perspective** where he would watch himself from the stands performing the perfect race from start to finish.

In addition, Bowman set up a "trigger" that would allow Phelps to enter this visualization pattern anytime he wanted to. What Bowman did was tell Michael Phelps to "put in the videotape" during training sessions. The videotape was the 3D IMAX movie Phelps played in his head before his practices and events.

So, every morning and every evening, Michael Phelps would watch his mental videotape and see everything in extreme detailed clarity and at a level of success. Even going beyond that, Michael Phelps would mentally train not only for the perfect situations, but also for situations where things were not perfect. Bowman described that Michael would even visualize situations where he may have a failure with his goggles.

Let's examine an Olympic race that he had in Beijing in 2008. Immediately after the race after coming off the start block, Michael Phelps described that he knew something was immediately wrong and noticed moisture building up in his goggles. He stated that as he approached the third turn of the race his goggles were completely filled with water.

Now this potentially could throw off many racers because seeing where you are is critical during the race. Despite this happening, Phelps had the advantage of visualization on his side. He had previously visualized himself having adverse events occurring, such as a goggle failure, and when it happened he described that he continued to swim calmly. Not only did Phelps mentally prepare for this but his coach had also trained him physically by making him swim in the dark during some of his training sessions because he wanted to prepare him for the most extreme situations.

So, as he continued to swim, being blind in the water, Phelps visualized his race plan and began to count his strokes, knowing down to the exact number exactly how many he would need before he touched the wall for the final time.

Not only did Michael Phelps win the race that day but he also set a world record.

When he was asked how it felt to swim blind, his response was simply:

"Like I imagined it would."

So, what I encourage you to do is to create your own "mental videotape" of having the ideal situation or event that you were striving for. Like Phelps, this is a tape that you want to play in your mind in the morning time and in the evening time, doing it daily to create that mental habit of repetition. And you want this tape in exquisite detail, seeing yourself take on the challenge with absolute perfection.

By doing this, you are mentally building victories within your mindset, so that as you start to achieve the small successes physically, they will begin to compound, enhance, and augment your mental preparation.

Enhancing Your Physical Reaction to Fear

This represents the transition from focusing on your mental training to your physical training. This involves preparing your body in advance for the physical manifestations of success.

Now, you are going to create a mental videotape that will help you overcome your fears. This will focus on relaxing you physically so when the fear occurs, you play the tape which will help relax you. The best time to use your mental videotape would be before you do the act that triggers the fear in the first place. Doing it this way will be more powerful for you.

Make sure you are in a well-lighted room but nothing that is too bright that it will irritate your eyes.

Let's begin!

Focus on an object straight ahead of you.

Now, the obvious question is, "How do I read this book and focus on the object at the same time?" What I would like you to do is read the passage first then put the book down and repeat the process as you focus on the object. You can simplify the process by recording the exercise to follow and listening to your voice on the tape. If you can't do that, I will provide a "cheat sheet" for you at the end of the exercise for you to reflect upon.

As you begin to look at the object, sitting down with your feet on the floor, you are going to begin to realize that you are much more relaxed and calmer now. You can begin to see the light or object slowly fading away as you begin to relax.

You feel a sense of calm and peace as time passes by.

You begin to visualize yourself becoming successful and having no fear or worry of the event that troubles you. Floating above yourself and as you look down at yourself completing the task, you see yourself encountering the challenges and watch yourself overcome them.

You hear yourself talking to yourself, saying one to two C.A.L.M.I.N.G. statements that keep you relaxed and calm. You tell yourself, "I'm confident I can do this," and, "Now is the time to act."

You feel the tension leaving your body as you become more successful, feeling your breath slow down and becoming more relaxed. The tension is slowly leaving your shoulders as you feel them drop down and you feel your feet sink deeper into the floor.

You begin to see your breathing going slowly in and out, calm and relaxed and as you listen even more closely you begin to hear that soft pattern rhythmically going in and out.

Taking a deep breath in slowly and you hold for one, two, and three and then you slowly breathe out in reverse three, two, and one feeling great and wonderful in every way.

Repeat this again a second time taking a breath slowly and now you're going to take that breath in for five starting with one, two, three, four, and five and then you slowly breathe out in reverse five, four, three, two, one feeling great and wonderful in every way.

You now focus on your heart rate, which is beating normally, and as you continue to sit and slowly breathe at a relaxed pace, you can begin to feel your heart rate becoming more relaxed and starting to slow down.

Floating above yourself, looking down at you completing the task successfully, you can see yourself doing it without any stress or fear, breathing at a normal pace and your heart rate is strong and steady.

You see yourself finishing the task, excited, patting yourself on the back for a job well done.

You flow back down into your body and you begin to feel even more relaxed and calm. You begin to feel exhilarated and excited, breathing at a normal pace, and seeing and hearing your heart rate calm and relaxed.

It's time for another deep breath. Take a breath in for three, starting with one, two, three and then you begin to exhale slowly backwards three, two, one, feeling great and relaxed.

One more final breath in for five counting in one, two, three, four, five and then slowly breathing out in reverse five, four, three, two, one.

As you are sitting down, you are feeling relaxed and finishing your final calming breaths, you begin to realize that you are relaxed and calm and successful because you can overcome your fear at any time that you choose.

How are you feeling right now?

Do you feel like your breathing is relaxed and at a calm pace?

Is your heart rate slow and steady?

Do you feel that you are less tense and less stressed overall?

As you continue to sit and reflect on the exercise of making your videotape, you are going to begin to feel the sensations that accompany calm, deep breathing, a strong heart rate, and low levels of tension—you are going to remember this is an anchor point on how you feel as you are overcoming your fears.

You can have a printed copy of this script by going to:

https://www.docdeliversbooks.com/free-ebook/

and scroll down to the section called "Visualization with Breathing."

I want you to really focus on the bodily sensations that you have now and to truly evaluate where you are at. What we are doing is we are creating an anchor for you to return to physically whenever you are playing your mental videotape, either routinely twice per day or five to 10 minutes before taking on the fearful event.

Remember the room that you were in as you did this and remember the object or the light that you focused on because you can use this is an anchor point wherever you are to practice the visualization technique wherever you go.

Understand that what we have just done is anchored your visualization or your mental videotape with physical sensations of being calm and relaxed. Thus, the combination of visualization and physical relaxation will be your powerful tool to utilize.

So, let me summarize what we just went through so that you can have your cheat sheet to take with you wherever you are:

1. Sit down upright with your feet on the ground, comfortable.

2. Focus on a light or an object in front of you.

3. Imagine the light or the object and as you continue to stare at it slowly, it fades away into the background and you begin to close your eyes.

4. Sounds in the background fade out and you only hear yourself talking.

5. Flow out of your body and watch yourself below, overcoming the fear.

6. Say one or two C.A.L.M.I.N.G. statements to yourself within your mind.

7. Focus on your body becoming more relaxed and less tense.

8. Focus on your breathing, becoming more relaxed, and take a deep breath in for three seconds and then exhale for three seconds.

9. Repeat your breathing, taking in a deep breath for five seconds and then exhaling for five seconds.

10. Focus on your heart rate becoming more relaxed and starting to slow down.

11. As you are floating above, look down on yourself, seeing yourself complete the task and congratulating yourself.

12. Flow back down into your body, feeling yourself relaxed, hearing your heartbeat calm, and feeling your breathing rate become slow and steady.

13. Breathe in for three seconds and out for three seconds.

14. Final deep breath in for five seconds and then out for five seconds.

15. Count backwards from three and once you hit one open your eyes.

16. Anchor in the feeling and remember how you are feeling relaxed right now, remembering your breath rate and your heart rate.

Again, you can get this shortened cheat sheet and the full script at:

https://www.docdeliversbooks.com/free-ebook/

and scroll down to the section called "Visualization with Breathing."

As I stated before, the key to this technique being successful is repetition.

Pay attention and begin to notice that you have a powerful visualization technique for yourself.

The first part of it is a multisensory visualization in the first person where you are seeing yourself overcome the task or event that causes you fear. Into this visualization, you can also build alternatives as to what can go wrong during the task or the event, so that you are mentally prepared to adjust for any variations that may occur.

The second portion of the 16 steps is more focused on looking at yourself from the third person and involves much more focus on the physical sensations of what you are feeling with your breath, heart rate, and level of tension. It is more of putting yourself in a meditative state and creating an anchor point that you can return to so that you can have sensations of feeling calm and relaxed physically during your event.

Now you have a powerful mental videotape so choose to use its components in the way that best resonates with you.

Remember, the most important thing is consistency and to do this each day.

Enhancing your definition of success

So far you have elevated your language, verified panic, verbalized calming, and visualized success while developing visualization techniques to evaluate and create a relaxed and calming state.

You have developed all the necessary tools to help you internally DO the things to overcome the fear but before we go into the next major section, which is taking action on your fear, there is one more mental tool that needs to be developed and that is how you visualize success.

Essentially, all of us have seen success at one time or another at one point of our lives, no matter how big or small. But there are two aspects of success that need to be further broken down before we begin to get to the next module of taking action.

First, the two questions that you ask yourself are:

"Am I feeling successful before I start to take action?"

"Is my definition of success too complicated to be realistic?"

The time frame of success

The issue that can derail people from overcoming fear and not achieving the things that they desire in their lives is that they look at success as a destination and not a journey.

What I commonly see is that people define themselves as successful once the task, goal, or outcome is complete. They work hard along the way, overcoming the fears and challenges in their journey. It is only after they reach the end point that they see themselves as successful. For them, success is all or none. They are not successful during the journey, only once they complete it.

The problem with this approach is that success is seen as an all or none and by having this mental attitude, people will see themselves as a failure if they do not achieve the outcome that they desire. If they fall short of your goal while having this mindset, they may see themselves as a failure and not as a success. Having feelings of failure could make it more challenging to get back up and make another run at the goal that they desire.

Therefore, their time frame of success is based on a **future** outlook.

Pay attention, because this is very important in the understanding of success.

Success is not based on a **future** outlook, success is based on your **present** outlook.

The optimal way to set yourself up for success is to have the mindset that you are successful now, **before you even take on the task or DO the steps to overcome the fear.**

So why is it important to have a mindset of success right now as opposed to delayed gratification and waiting for it later? Because when you are adopting this mindset of delayed gratification, you are not appreciating the fact that you are indeed successful right now.

The very fact that you are reading this and learning the techniques that I have presented will help you realize that you are already successful now. You are taking the steps to move your life in the direction of overcoming your fears and achieve the outcomes that you desire.

Therefore, you are successful now even before you have started the actual act of trying to overcome the fear!

Do you realize this!

And there are many more benefits of having a present mindset of success as opposed to a future mindset of success. Let's take a look at the chart below to compare success now and later so that you will begin to understand the importance of this concept and the mindset that you need to develop.

Having a *future* mindset of success:	Having a *present* mindset of success:
Delay of gratification and no fuel to keep your forward momentum	Not delaying gratification and having the fuel of momentum
Seeing the outcome as a final event that has a point of termination	Seeing the outcome is a continuous path to success that does not end
Not appreciating your progress	Appreciating your progress
Having no visual or verbal foundation to build on	Having a visual and verbal foundation that stacks and compounds
Losing the momentum if you encounter a setback	Maintaining the momentum if you encounter a setback
Feeling empty if you fall short of the outcome	Feeling fulfilled despite falling short of the outcome
Relies on completion of the outcome	Does not rely on completion of the outcome

No triggers to assess if your path is still congruent with your values	Triggers are present to assess if your path is still congruent with your values
More obsession with the endpoint	More obsession with the journey
Creates a one and done mentality	Not an all or none mentality but a continuous line for success

Table 1: the time frame of success, future versus present

So, let's review this table in more detail to have a better understanding of the importance of having a mindset that is present instead of a mindset of the future.

Do you remember the visualization technique when you were floating above your body and watching yourself pat yourself on the back?

Now you'll begin to understand the importance of that, the importance of self-congratulation. By congratulating yourself over the small victories and progress that you have made and continuing to add to your stores of confidence that will compound over time, you will begin overtaking the underlying fear.

Your overall job with overcoming the fear is to act first, from a physical standpoint. By taking that action, you are slowly, over time, building your mental confidence through the small victories that you will achieve. And as you have small victories, continue to congratulate yourself, and see your success it will continue to add the fuel and momentum that will sustain your path towards achieving the outcome in overcoming the fear.

Think of it in this way:

Would you rather make a six-hour trip in the car that you have never been in the driver's seat of before, not knowing the fuel mileage that you can get, and hope that you can reach your destination on a single tank of gas? Or, would you rather make that same six-hour trip in this unfamiliar vehicle and stop every two hours, stretch to reflect on the fun of the journey, and fill the tank back up?

Because what can happen during this trip is that you can run into traffic, get a flat tire, have to take bathroom breaks, or just get physically tired and need a short break.

Like life, you may run into traffic in the form of obstacles or setbacks or you may get mentally fatigued during your journey. However, if you are constantly filling your tank and have the satisfaction that you are maximizing your efforts for success, you significantly increase your chances that you will reach your destination.

And that brings us to our next point where you see the outcome as a final event and termination. That is having the mindset that you're only happy when you have reached your destination. Success is a continuous journey, like our journey in the car. It's kind of like you driving through multiple states and taking the time to stop, sightsee, and enjoy the ride. The success is not in the destination but in the journey and adventure towards your outcome.

Successes are the waypoints that allow you to sustain the ride. As you feel more successful, you get less discouraged and appreciate more of what you have already accomplished.

Appreciating the progress that you have made helps you to reflect upon why you decided to take this journey in the first place. The small victories that you achieve build up over time. As you continue to drive forward, you are not only overcoming your fear but growing into a more powerful and successful version of you.

As you're driving along on your journey, the visualizations that you have built in your mind are becoming a manifestation of your physical being. As you begin to overcome the fear and see that you are successful now, you begin to appreciate the little things, the little steps that are transforming you physically.

The further you go along your journey, you become a little less stressed and a little more relaxed. You begin to realize that you're not as anxious and you appreciate that you are breathing more calmly and effectively. You begin to see the small little steps that you have overcome.

Where would this be helpful? Say you're driving in your car and you get a flat tire. Now, if you haven't been appreciating the journey and have no success to build upon, you may get frustrated at this point, which can derail your entire trip because you don't have a mindset that will help get you over the obstacle. But, if you've been developing small victories and have that mindset of success along the journey, you might recall the beautiful sites that you see and appreciate the obstacles that you have overcome. You'll begin to have more drive for completing the journey because of your desire to experience even the small victories along the way.

So, by having the mindset of success, you are not feeling empty at this point because you have visual and physical memories and victories to fall back on, which in turn means that you don't have to rely on getting to your destination. Obviously, that is the endpoint, to completely overcome the fear and have an outcome of completion. However, it's not necessary because you are already successful now because of the small victories that you have built and the roads that you've already traveled.

When you feel yourself on the sidelines, like that car with a flat tire, it gives you that time to reflect, that time to think about how far your journey has taken you. It's like double checking your GPS to make sure that you're still on the right track. It's like double checking your core values to make sure that the path that you are on is still congruent with the initial core values that you established for yourself. You can ask yourself, "Are my small victories and levels of success now continuing to grow me into the person I choose to be?"

By having this time to reflect upon your journey, by having a mindset of being successful right now and not waiting for it in the future, you will begin to discover and appreciate that success is all about the journey. It's about taking the small steps of success, one by one, building upon them and appreciating that every time you drive forward one more inch, one more mile. Success is within you now and your outcome is just a greater manifestation of what you're experiencing today.

After understanding the importance of success, you will now define it within your own life. Take the time to create your personalized definition of success, specifically when it comes to overcoming a fear that you may have. Later, you will simplify it to make it more workable and obtainable for you!

For example, if you have a fear of talking with people and your overall outcome is to promote your new business, you may have a definition such as:

"I will be successful when I talk to people more confidently, they buy my products, I make more sales, and I am happy with the services that I provide other people."

Did you come up with your definition?

Webster defines success simply as "a favorable or desired outcome."

Now let's go back to the example that I put in as far as a definition of success which was:

"I will be successful when I talk to people more confidently, they buy my products, I make more sales, and I am happy with the services that I provide other people."

Pay attention to the statement and look very closely. Notice that the statement of success doesn't have a **single** desired outcome, it has **multiple outcomes.**

There is the outcome of talking more confidently.

There is the outcome of people buying products.

There is the outcome of being happy with the services that I provide.

When looking at the above example, success is defined when three different outcomes occur.

Essentially what you're doing is you're complicating your definition of success because instead of having success based off one outcome your success is based off three outcomes. Let's simplify this definition and then your own one.

Follow closely because this is a very important concept to grasp.

With this example then, as you progress through the steps in overcoming your fear, say you can talk to people more confidently, people buy more of your products but you're not quite happy with the level of service that you provide. You've only met two of the three components of your personalized definition of success. Because you are not happy you did not fulfill all the requirements of your definition of success.

Thus, you are essentially saying that you are not successful.

Does that make sense?

It may sound like a picky point, but we have already established the importance of language, so the definition that you are planting within your subconscious is critical. You're essentially telling your subconscious you are not successful because you have not met all the criteria based off your own definition of success.

This example definition of success is stacked with so many outcomes. You are tripling the necessary things that must occur to meet your level of success. What is this doing in the long run? It adds more stress because now there are multiple things that you must be or do to be successful.

Is this really the definition that you want for yourself?

Do you want so many events to work in your favor before you call yourself a success?

Are you looking to have a definition of success that will put the odds in your favor of fulfilling it and truly being successful?

There are two ways that you can modify this in order to define success in terms that make it far more favorable for you to achieve it.

One, you can modify your definition of success that includes one outcome. For example, we can say:

"I am successful when I talk more confidently."

"I'm successful when more people buy my products."

"I'm successful when I am happy with the services that I provide."

Now, this will simplify your definition of success, however, it limits your potential because now you can only be successful when a single outcome occurs. You are telling yourself success in your life is only based on one outcome.

It's a pretty limited outlook.

The trick is to have success built in a way that doesn't require having to achieve multiple outcomes yet preserves the option for you to be successful with multiple outcomes.

Let's say that again, you are going to create a definition of success for yourself that can be more easily achieved while still having a variety of outcomes.

This is much simpler than it sounds, and it only requires one simple word, two simple letters.

It is a strategy that I learned from one of my powerful mentors, Michael Bernoff, and involves just a small tweak by adding this one simple word:

OR

That's it!

Let's put this into practical application.

Here is our original definition of success:

"I will be successful when I talk to people more confidently, they buy my products, and I am happy with the services that I provide other people."

Now, let's modify the definition of success by adding the word *or.*

*"I will be successful when I talk to people more confidently, **or** they buy my products, **or** I am happy with the services that I provide other people."*

Do you see the difference?

You are preserving your original definition of success, while giving yourself options and having multiple avenues of success without the stress of having to fulfill all those outcomes in order to be successful.

So, with our modified definition, if I talk to people more confidently, I'm successful.

If people buy my products and I'm happy with the services that I provide, I'm successful.

If the people simply buy my products, then I'm successful.

Can you see how adding the powerful word "or" allows you to have a definition of success that is much more simplified and easier to achieve?

Now, you are applying this in your module for overcoming fear, but this can easily be applied to any aspect of life that you have.

For example, when I focus on my health, my definition of success is:

*"I'm successful when I eat healthy meals the majority of the day, **or** I work out for the day, **or** I drink my six glasses of water, **or** I don't eat junk food throughout the day, **or** I do my weightlifting, **or** I do my stretching."*

Yes, it's a long sentence and written this way on purpose. The point is that success doesn't have to be a laundry list of items. You can be successful once you achieve any *one* of these. You are successful with working out. Or, you could be successful by lifting weights, and so on.

Now I am training my subconscious that I'm successful if I achieve one of any of the six outcomes within my definition of success.

Going back to the overall theme of fear, say you have a fear of flying.

You can have a definition of success in overcoming your fear of flying such as:

*"I successfully overcome my fear of flying when I sit on the plane and strap on my seatbelt, **or** I practice my visualization for five minutes, **or** I practice my deep breathing for two minutes, **or** I can look out the window and feel calm, **or** I can laugh to myself on the plane, **or** I successfully walk off the plane at the end of the flight."*

So now you have a success definition for overcoming your fear of flying when you meet any of these criteria.

Can you see what we're doing at this point?

You are physically and mentally creating small successes that will continue to stack up and help overcome your fear of flying.

This is how you optimize your definition of success, by using the linkage word "or," allowing you to have success as you achieve small mini successes, still meet your definition while preserving multiple avenues for success.

Now that you have a strong definition of success, you equally must have a strong definition of failure. You must be honest, if you are here at this point, then you may have had events in your life where you haven't felt successful or have had an overwhelming mindset of failure. That as well can be modified with the use of a linking word and in this case that would be:

AND

Again, another powerful concept learned from my mentor Michael Bernoff.

What you're going to do is create a powerful definition of failure that is so complex it essentially makes failure impossible to achieve. By using the linking word "and," so many events will need to occur in order to achieve failure that it will be impossible to get there.

Going back to the subject of having a fear of flying, an example of doing this would be the following:

"I have failed to overcome my fear of flying as I frequently and regularly, time and time again, stress every single day for a minimum of eight hours a day for 30 days straight before I even have the flight, ***and*** *I get on the flight and have a panic attack for the entire flight,* ***and*** *I get out of my seat multiple times during the flight because I am nervous,* ***and*** *I don't look out of the window one time during the flight,* ***and*** *I never have a happy thought anytime during the entire flight,* ***and*** *I am so panicked at the end of the flight that I have to be wheelchaired off of the flight,* ***and*** *I forget to realize how simplistic and satisfying my definition of success with flying is."*

Now this definition means that so many insane things must happen for me to define it as a failure. When you use a time frame such as the eight hours for 30 days, you want to use time frames that are so unrealistic that it would be essentially impossible to achieve. And when compared to the definition of success, you want to have many more outcomes for failure so that you would have to achieve ***every single outcome*** in order to fulfill your definition of failure.

The powerful component of your definition of failure is that at the end because you are adding the fact that you remember how simplistic and satisfying it is to meet your definition of success. So, it forces you to think upon your definition of success, allowing you to do one small outcome within that success definition, moving you further away from the mindset of failure.

Take a piece of paper because you are going to create your two definitions: success and failure.

First, you are going to create your powerful definition of success by utilizing the linking word "or."

Second, you are going to create your powerful definition of failure by utilizing the linking word "and."

Once you have them written down, I would encourage you to post your definitions in a location that you can visualize every day at your home or workplace. What I like to do is have a miniaturized version of my definitions that I can pull out of my wallet anytime that I need it.

Take the next 30 minutes to create your two powerful definitions.

With regards to the definitions, I really want you to think outside of the box and have a minimum of 15 different outcomes for each one. The more the better, especially when it comes to the definition of failure.

Your definition of success, by using the word "or" will be true when any *one* of the outcomes have been achieved. It **simplifies** a definition of success where multiple events can occur for success to happen.

Your definition of failure, by using the word "and" will be true when *all* the outcomes have been achieved. It **complicates** a definition of failure because everything needs to go wrong for you to call yourself a failure. That's a good thing!

To download the worksheets for this exercise, simply go to:

https://www.docdeliversbooks.com/free-ebook/

and scroll down to the section called "Success and Failures Definitions."

F.E.A.R. (Taking action to overcome fear)

We are now in the third phase of the fear cycle and it is time to act!

After building the mental and visual foundation, it is time to move forward physically by taking action. As we stated in the beginning, when one is trying to overcome their fears, action is the necessary first step that must be taken.

Let's review again the algorithm that represents this:

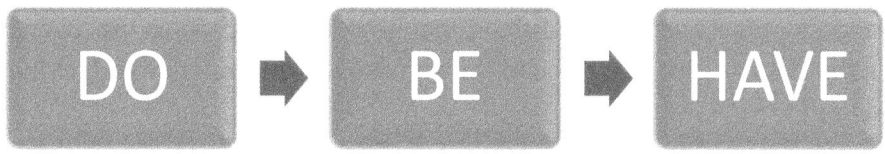

The correct model for overcoming fear

Again, we're acting first, because we may not have the mindset that works from a high level of confidence. Thus, we must utilize action as a necessary first step to move towards overcoming the fear.

You are going to learn how to act:

The R.I.G.H.T. Way

Taking the R.I.G.H.T. Action

Here are all the different components of that and we will further break them down:

R – resilient

I – instantaneous

G – grateful

H – harmonious

T – time efficient

Action that is Resilient

Do you remember the story of Braveheart? It was the 1995 movie that was directed by Mel Gibson who starred as William Wallace, leader of the Scottish people, fighting against England and King Edward I in the first war of Scottish independence. Now, given the fact that this occurred in the late 13th century, we may not have the most accurate records of the true events of that time; however, we can use the legend in the story as a teaching tool to show the power of resiliency and taking action.

In the battle of Sterling Bridge, the Scottish Army, which had a strength of approximately 6000 men, had to face the superior British Army with the strength of 9000 soldiers. Among these numbers, The Scottish Army had 300 cavalry compared to 2000 for the British. With the British having thousands of more soldiers and almost seven times more horsemen, the odds were in their favor that day.

The Scottish Army could've decided to flee that day given the overwhelming odds against them. However, they remained resilient and decided to take action nevertheless. In the end, the Battle of Sterling Bridge resulted in victory for the Scottish Army.

When faced with fear or odds that seem against you, you must be resilient in your action. At the time of that battle between the Scottish and English, the Scottish were able to remain resilient because of their desire for independence. Essentially, their "why" was powerful enough for them to remember why they decided to step on a battlefield in the first place.

It is the same thing that you must do in order to remain resilient and act despite the fear. You'll develop the tools to do so because you have created an empowered you with your own personal "why" and by proposing the initial three questions to you:

"What have I lost out on in my life because of fear?"

"Am I open to looking at my fear in a different way?"

"Am I ready to take the necessary steps to start to challenge and overcome my fear?"

So, as you begin to act, it is essential to be resilient. There are going to be times along the way where you may either struggle with taking that initial action or maintaining the momentum as you engage in the action. These are the times to remember the lesson of defining your why that is seven levels deep.

The Webster's definition of resilience is *"an ability to recover from or adjust easily to a misfortune or change."*

During your journey, you've learned multiple techniques that will help you overcome fear. And as you progress in overcoming it, you will become more resilient because of it.

One of the main tools is utilizing your powerful visualization technique and already seeing yourself being successful despite the challenges and setbacks.

Another tool that you have developed is utilizing your language pattern with yourself and identifying the fear as you feel it coming on. And as you start to P.A.N.I.C. and recognized fear is coming on, you can use one of your C.A.L.M.I.N.G. statements that will help diminish the power of fear and maintain your resiliency.

The third major tool is the creation of your powerful statements of success and failure. Armed with these statements, you can retain your resiliency knowing that it only takes one small outcome to be successful but many more outcomes to be a failure. There is resiliency built within the statement of success because as it was stated many times in the past, it only takes one small act of success to build the foundation and continue to forge forward.

Action is instantaneous

Nike said it best:

"Just Do It."

Let's face it, there are many people that like to plan and think and then plan some more and overthink some more, eventually getting to a point where they turn from a mindset of action to a mindset of inaction. The direct opposite is required when taking on the challenge of overcoming fear because the longer you try to plan, analyze, and think the situation through, the more time you give yourself to let your emotions overcome your ability to act.

That's why action must be instantaneous.

When I talk about instantaneous action, I want you to focus more on the act itself, or the physical component, as opposed to the thinking or mental component. Remember, you are looking to overcome your fears first by building your physical actions which in turn will develop the confidence that you'll need to sustain it. And remember this, any action is a massive success because you are creating the habit and the mindset within your subconscious. If you can overcome fear in a small way and push yourself a little bit further the next time you try to overcome it, you are building many events of success and accomplishment. They will continue to compound as you continue to act going forward.

Action is momentum and every time you act you are creating forward momentum. As you are creating momentum you are becoming successful. And as you become more successful you build your confidence and then, as you build your confidence, you take further action.

Imagine it as a never-ending loop that works in your favor and continues to build and intensify.

It's like the ice skater that starts their stationary spin on the ice. It starts very slowly, however, as they continue to spin in place, the momentum they build allows them to spin even faster, eventually turning with less energy as time goes on.

That is what we're building with you!

You are creating slow and study actions that will lead to success. That will build your belief within yourself and strengthen your confidence, turning it into an automatic, repetitive process that only stops if you choose to allow it to.

Action supported with gratitude

In a previous module, we talked about having to express gratitude after you have physically completed the action that was taken to overcome your fear. Now, you are going to begin to use that gratitude in the real world.

With regards to gratitude, it is not only important to be grateful that you completed the action that allowed you to conquer your fear and slowly build your confidence, but you also must be grateful for even having the courage to take the action in the first place. In your case, be grateful in the fact that you choose to grow and move towards the outcomes that you desire.

I'm a strong believer in gratitude because it is linked with another entity that I believe in and that is the Law of Attraction.

I personally journal my gratitude in various aspects of my life every morning during my morning ritual. The journaling of gratitude allows me to appreciate the courage that I had to take on the challenges of yesterday and maintain the gratitude to have the strength to take on the new challenges of today.

I truly believe that it is very challenging to move forward and have the things that you desire in your future if you don't appreciate what you have in your present. Learn to appreciate your actions even before you take them, patting yourself on the back for taking the steps to overcome your fear or enhance your life in whatever way that you choose. For example, if your challenge is to overcome a fear of public speaking, don't focus on the negative and the challenge that you have with overcoming your fear but have gratitude in knowing that you are taking the steps to do so. And it could be a step as simple as saying hello to a colleague and having a 30-second conversation, which you otherwise may not have engaged in.

The question I propose is this:

If you are not grateful for what you have at this current point in time, how do you expect to attract the things in your life that you desire?

So, no matter how small the action that you take, no matter how minuscule you may feel it is, if it is action that is moving you one step closer towards overcoming fear, that is something to be grateful about. And as you build your levels of gratitude, you will begin to realize that you attract more things in your life that will help you overcome the fear without you even asking for them. Simply, by being grateful, things come when you least expect them!

Action that is harmonious with your "why"

It's the action that you take that brings you closer to your overall outcome of overcoming your fear, but it is also action that is consistent with your underlying "why" and core values.

Let's use the following example:

You are taking on the challenge to overcome your fear of public speaking and the reason "why" you want to do it is because you want to become that person who inspires others to overcome their own fears of public speaking.

Let's also say that you have established the core values of confidence and compassion. Your way of being more confidence could involve talking with people in the office that you normally wouldn't talk to.

You have successfully taken action by the fact that you spoke with the person that you ordinarily wouldn't have talked with. However, imagine that the conversation that you had wasn't pleasant. Imagine that you put down and humiliated the person during your talk. Yes, you took action.

Do you think belittling and talking down to the person in the office was compassionate in any way? Yes, you took action to get more confidence but was it harmonious with your other core value of compassion?

And what about your core value of confidence?

You're going to move closer towards becoming more confident, but you're doing it at the expense of other core values that you have. Make sure that if you have a defined set of core values, you are able to act upon all of them without conflict. One thing not to do is to express one core value at the expense of another. In our above example, you are more confident, but your confidence is at the expense of losing your compassion for another person.

Action that is time efficient

When we talk about action that is time efficient, there are two main components that you must utilize in order to maximize the effort that you put forward in the first place. These two things are:

1. Focusing on action that has quality and is not filled with quantity.

2. The maximum amount of action in the shortest amount of time.

These two areas of time efficiency focus on three well-established principles, which are:

1. Pomodoro Technique

2. Pareto's principle

3. Parkinson's law

We are going to focus on the first principle which is the **Pomodoro Technique**.

This technique was developed by Francesco Cirillo in the 1980s as his personalized system in order to get more studying done. It works by going through an alternating cycle of doing work and then taking short breaks in between. It's a phenomenal way to be more efficient and you can see what else they have to offer at:

https://francescocirillo.com/pages/pomodoro-technique

The basic concept is that you choose the task that you wish to get done, set a time limit of 25 minutes (in the traditional model but since its original creation it has been modified) and then taking a five-minute break after which, you repeat the 30-minute cycle again.

This can be done up to four cycles or two hours at which time you would take a longer break such as a half an hour.

Now, how can you apply this to taking action in overcoming our fears?

By putting yourself up against the clock and knowing that you have a limited amount of time to take action will give you less time to potentially overthink a situation or involve your emotions. That will take you from a state of inaction to becoming more open about taking action. Knowing that your time is limited will help mentally drive you towards taking action that is not only instantaneous, but for the purpose of this section, is efficient.

This entire section on overcoming fear was done using this exact method! When I set the timer for myself (and I do 50-minute sessions with a 10-minute break), I found that I was a lot more efficient because I was hyper focused in that 50-minute session. Even more importantly, I had less time to overthink, procrastinate or be fearful about what I was going to put in this specific section because I knew that I was up against the clock. So, it can work beautifully with overcoming fear and taking action because you know that action must be done within a specific time frame.

Pareto's principle, which is also known as the 80/20 rule, states that approximately 80% of your results are going to come from 20% of your actions. It was suggested by management consultant Joseph M. Juran and named after the Italian economist Vilfredo Pareto.

The importance of this concept is understanding that not everything that you do is going to be the most efficient use of your time. Thus, the actions that you take in overcoming your fear need to be carefully scrutinized. So, you need to ask yourself what things or actions am I doing that are going to be the most productive for overcoming my fears?

Are you doing actions that are truly an efficient and productive use of your time? Are you doing actions that make you feel good but don't move you forward because they are simply fluff that you took upon yourself in order to not do the real actions that you may be fearful of?

So, by not doing the right type of action, you take yourself further away from overcoming your fear and you are cheating yourself by doing things that you know are unproductive or you may not see as unproductive.

Going back to our example of public speaking, one of the actions that we may take to overcome this fear would be to have a 30-minute conversation with a close friend or have a deeper conversation with a spouse. Now, these are both actions that focus on communication, however, it's not the type of communication that you are looking for because likely these are people that you already feel comfortable speaking with. This would be an example of doing 80% of the action that's only going to get you 20% of the results that you're trying to obtain.

But if you are looking to get 80% of the results with just 20% of your actions, you may set up the challenge to take action and speak to one new person in your department at work or take a new Toastmasters class and give a five-minute icebreaker speech. Now these actions are outside your comfort zone because you're talking to new people and they're going to give you more results and more efficiently get you closer to the overall outcome that you are seeking to achieve.

So, listen closely and remember this:

Action is great, but you must take effective action.

Finally, let's talk a little bit about **Parkinson's law**, created by Cyril Parkinson within his published essay in "The Economist" in 1955.

Parkinson's law states that, "Work expands so as to fill the time available for its completion."

In layman's terms, for example, if you gave yourself one week to do a one-hour task, then the task will increase in complexity to the point that it will require that entire week to get it complete. And that doesn't necessarily mean that you will spend all that working week to complete the one-hour task. During that week, you may lose time because of frustration, significantly increasing the complexity of the task, or feeling overwhelmed, stressed, or fearful.

This hinders you in your desire to act towards achieving your goals because now you have greatly expanded the time to do a very short task. And when you have that extra time to complete the task, then you can fill that time with more thoughts of P.A.N.I.C. and less thoughts that are C.A.L.M.I.N.G. That gives away significant blocks of time that can otherwise be used to overcome the fear in the first place.

So, let's use Parkinson's law to our advantage then!

If we apply Parkinson's law towards shorter time frames, the same principles will apply. Looking at our example on the opposite end of the spectrum, say we only give ourselves 20 minutes to complete the one-hour task. What you will come to discover is that you will manage to find the time in 20 minutes to complete that one-hour task because you are working more effectively, efficiently, and not increasing the overall complexity of the task at hand.

Now the advantage of having the shorter time frame is that you have less time overall to brainstorm or to think things through in a negative way. You know that the job must be done and there is no time to waste. As you work faster and more efficiently, you will begin to discover that you have less time to be fearful about the task and more time to focus on achieving it.

Think about this in your own life where you waited to the last minute to do a task or assignment. When crunch time hit, you were able to pack a significant amount of work into a very small amount of time.

In conclusion, when you think about time efficiency remember these three principles:

Focus on small blocks of time to maximize your efficiency.

Focus on the actions that give you the greatest results.

Focus on a time frame that is compressed enough to allow you not to mismanage it or overcomplicate the action.

In the next section of the F.E.A.R. Cycle, you are coming to the fourth and final step. This step is not only important for self-reflection but for making the connection back to your initial start point of "*FOCUS,*" allowing you to work in a continuous loop that in time, will become self-sustaining and continue to move you forward towards overcoming your fear.

F.E.A.R. (Recall, Reassess and Reengage)

If you are at the stage that you have taken the first action step towards overcoming your fears, congratulations to you!

If not, no worries, I will get you there!

This stage is critical because after the action is taken, understand that this is just the first of many steps towards helping you to overcome your fears. Think of the steps as a never-ending cycle that continues to move in a clockwise direction, always going through the four stages.

Essentially, this is the checkpoint stage where you are evaluating everything that you have done up to this time and preparing yourself to successfully take another spin of the next F.E.A.R. Cycle.

Recalling the actions that you have taken is a critical step for analyzing what you have done and how to make it better. There are two main reasons for recalling them:

Recall (reason #1)

The recall stage is a reflection of your C.A.L.M.I.N.G. statement and it's important to use it in this area for two reasons.

After you have done the act to help you overcome the fear, you may be in a state where you are excited or exhilarated, and this is the perfect time to reinforce that behavior. This would be the time to restate and reinforce your power statement of success.

As a reminder, here are the C.A.L.M.I.N.G. statements that I have already created for you:

"I'm Confident that I can...."

"I take Action today to get closer to the outcomes tomorrow."

"Life becomes more exciting as I grow out of my fear."

"Memories of success are within me."

"I can do anything for…"

"Now is the time to Act."

"Growth is what I strive for, each and every day."

If you have a statement or statements that are easier for you to remember, then definitely feel free to use them.

However, when crafting your power statements be very careful to avoid certain combinations of words, especially those that don't make the statement definitive or make the statement a forced event.

For example, these would be statement such as:

"I have to…"

"I must…"

"I should…"

The first two statements are those that can give your subconscious the implication that this is something that is forced and truly doesn't resonate with what you really want to do.

The third statement is not definitive because it gives the option that something should be done but doesn't necessarily have to be done.

A more optimal statement that you would utilize would be:

"I choose to…"

When you say I choose to, you are making a statement that this is an action that you chose of your own free will; no one else committed you to this choice.

Also, if you are looking to draft your own set of power statements, take care to note that:

1. They include only **positive** affirmations. For example, instead of saying, "I choose to not be scared to fly anymore," you would say, "I choose to overcome my fear of flying."

    A very subtle difference but powerful change.

2. They include one statement of **action**. For example, stating, "Each time that I fly, I become more confident."

3. They include one statement of **success**. For example, you could state, "Every time I visualize flying, I become more successful in overcoming it."

Not only do you want to use your power statements immediately after you take action, you also want to make sure that you do it twice a day, preferably in the mornings and evenings because you are creating an anchor for a successful F.E.A.R. Cycle. Having completed the first cycle, you've created an anchor of support that will allow you to flow through the next cycle even more effectively and efficiently.

Recall (reason #2)

The second reason for stating your power statement will be in situations where you may not have had the ideal results of the actions that you took on. Despite having your prewritten statements of success and failure, you may have an action that you feel is not up to par with your desired level of progress. The perfect time to use a power statement is when you have a negative mindset.

That is the exact reason why we have our power statements as words of positive affirmation which include statements of action and statements of success. This is because you always want to acknowledge that taking any action, despite it not being the outcome that you desired, is still successful.

Understand this, *success does not come from you having a successful action, success comes from you taking the action in the first place.* Think of the success of the action as a bonus but don't take away from your courage to do the action in the first place!

Reassess

During the reassessment portion of this phase, there are three main questions that you will ask yourself. They are:

"What did I do correctly?"

"What did I do incorrectly?"

"What is my opportunity to excel?"

"What did I do correctly?"

It is very important to recognize the things that went right and not take them for granted. These are the things that you especially want to focus on because they are going to be the actions that will get you the most beneficial results. Go back to thinking about Pareto's principle. These actions, if taken correctly, are potentially going to be part of the 20% of actions that get you 80% of the results. It doesn't mean that every action that you take correctly is going to be beneficial for you in the long run, but it will provide you with the start to analyze those things that are successful.

"What did I do incorrectly?"

When you are evaluating what you did incorrectly understand that you're not being critical of yourself. You are simply analyzing the things that did not go in your favor so that you can know what events should not be repeated.

Are you familiar with the definition of insanity?

One of the definitions is "doing the same thing over and over again and expecting different results."

Do not get into the habit of repeating incorrect actions that won't get you results. If you do this, you may continue along that same path because they are less fearful for you. You are better than that and you deserve much more than that. You're starting to slip from a person that takes action back to a person that is living inside their comfort zone and their "safe space."

So, some of the questions to ask yourself during this reassessment phase of what you did incorrectly would be:

"When fear arose, did I accept it or did I verify the P.A.N.I.C.?"

"Was the action that I took consistent with my level of visualized success?"

"Did I use proper visualization by playing the videotape in my head before I took on the task?"

"Did I use C.A.L.M.I.N.G. statements to help empower me?"

"Did I elevate my internal language and saturate it with positive thoughts?"

"Did I use the techniques to physically relax myself, slow down my breathing, my heart rate, and make myself less tense?"

"Did I have a mindset of success in the present or was I delaying my success to the future?"

There are many more questions that you can use for your assessment that you can tailor specifically to you. But utilize these as a starting point in the reassessment phase to understand how you may have fallen short of the desired outcome of that particular action.

"What is my opportunity to excel?"

Finally, you want to look at what I like to call "the opportunity to excel." This applies to both the things you did correctly and the things that you did incorrectly.

When you're looking at the actions that you did correctly the question to ask yourself is, "How can I even make this more successful than it already is?" Some of the questions to ask yourself are:

"How can I improve my mindset?"

"Can I make an adjustment with my power statement to make it more effective?"

"Can I create a visualization that is even more vivid, with more detail?"

"What action can I take that makes me feel even more comfortable that is even a step beyond what I just did?"

When you're looking at the actions that you did incorrectly, the question to ask yourself is "do I need to eliminate, modify or tweak this action so that it gives me a greater level of success?"

(Remember, you're already successful by doing the action even though you did not get the results that you wanted. I'm simply looking to make the actions more productive for you!)

Some of the questions to ask yourself are:

"Is this action congruent with my *why* and core values?"

"Was this action not successful because I failed to utilize my tools of visualization or power statements?"

"If this action was one that could be beneficial to me, how would it look if I executed it more effectively?"

Reengage

Your overall analysis of your actions and the mental and physical tools that you used before are going to be crucial towards improving upon yourself and having the next successful F.E.A.R. Cycle, bringing you closer towards overcoming the fear and achieving your outcomes.

The key to reengagement is preparing for the next F.E.A.R. Cycle and most importantly, preparing yourself visually, emotionally, and physically to repeat the steps that are necessary for overcoming the fear and achieving your outcome.

Understand this and pay attention closely because this is an important fact to remember.

You are not looking to eliminate the fear 100%.

If you could, if you were the type of person to achieve that feat, that would be outstanding! However, I believe that there must be an element of fear that remains because it continues to act as the catalyst to continue to improve and enhance yourself.

If you were without fear 100%, then what is your driving force to continue to improve yourself? What is your target or your focus to continue to strive to get a little bit better each day? For me, I still have a fear when I swim in the open waters during my triathlons and I have not eliminated it 100% nor do I choose to do so. The reason why is because as I step to the starting line, I harness the power of the fear which drives me through the F.E.A.R. Cycle and reminds me of all the tools that I have available to me not only to overcome the fear but to excel and drive past it at a level that I otherwise wouldn't do so.

So, as I prepare to reengage and go to the beginning of the cycle which starts with *focus,* I have a mental preparation of all the tools within my toolbox that will help carry me along the next cycle.

I remember to celebrate that I am successful with the last action that I took. Not necessarily because I achieved the small outcome from the action that I did but because I had the courage and the strength to do the action in the first place, despite the results.

I restate my "why," a statement so powerful that it empowers me to the point that not taking action not continuing to get better to overcome my fear is unforgivable.

I reflect upon my core values, so that I am constantly on track and taking action that is consistent with the person that I desire to be deep down.

I recall my powerful trifecta of statements which include:

My C.A.L.M.I.N.G. statement.

My statement for success.

My statement for failure.

I practice my visualization twice a day every day and incorporate it with a meditation that physically relaxes me, helps control my breathing, and slows down my heart rate to help alleviate any fear or panic.

And then I imagine taking the next step by using the R.I.G.H.T. Action. I operate in the physical state instead of the mental state, until which time that my confidence is built to the point that it equals and surpasses the physical actions that I have taken.

Going through the first round of the "F.E.A.R. Cycle"

Now, after reviewing all the components of the F.E.A.R. Cycle it's time for you to start incorporating them into your life. What I am referring to is this: You have mentally and physically done the things that will help you overcome the fear, moving forward towards the goals and outcomes that you desire.

Next, to bridge the gap between where you are now and where you want to be in the future, you will begin using even more powerful techniques of visualization.

Let's "SEE" the person that has the outcomes that you desire!

CHAPTER 10
YOUR THIRD TRIMESTER: SEE

What is visualization and why is it important?

Visualization is the process of using your mental capabilities to foresee a future event. I've only scratched the surface of it previously and now I will take it to the next level!

It involves the process of creating a picture within your mind that may or may not exist within your physical world. Most people who use visualization are trying to create a mental picture of an event or setting that typically doesn't exist within their reality at that time.

However, the term "visualization" is a misnomer, at least for our purposes. When using visualization to help you achieve your goals and outcomes, it involves way more than just the visual sense.

In order to develop the power of this technique, I will be guiding you to utilize all five of your senses. The key is to have a "visualization" that is so sensory rich, the subconscious mind can't and won't tell mental visualization from physical reality! When you visualize that your outcomes are already achieved, it will be a powerful leap that will catapult you closer towards physically achieving them.

How does visualization differ from dreams?

You may ask yourself, "Can't I just dream about success and call it a day? I just don't have the time to visualize and fantasize about stuff?"

First, visualization and dreams are completely different because they involve two distinctly different brain wave patterns. Alpha waves in our brain are used for visualization and Theta waves for sleep and the REM state. You can't **consciously control** our dreams because they exist in the Theta waves which is the realm of our subconscious (unless you're *lucid dreaming* and that's a book in itself!). However, you can **consciously influence** your subconscious by learning how to tap into your Alpha waves and implant the images, words, sounds, feelings, etc. that you want your subconscious brain to take a hold of.

We visualize all the time. The problem is that we simply don't use the technique to our advantage. When we dream, we don't have the flexibility of deciding what time frame we want to visualize in. The dreams are random and uncontrolled, for the most part. However, you can control through visualization, how our future looks. There are no rules or any limits towards visualization, they are simply a reflection of your level of creativity, so have fun with it.

Think about it: If I were to show you a way that you could implant images in your subconscious that your mind thought was real, do you think that it would help you move towards the goals and outcomes that you desire?

Absolutely!

What I teach you in this section are a set of tools to start the process of visualization. No worries if you haven't done it before, because you will start with simple techniques that you can start doing today.

Think of the brain as a muscle and if you haven't worked it before, it's going to take some time to get it strong (but not too much time!).

It's important to understand that your subconscious mind is like a bank that takes in what your conscious mind deposits. Some of these deposits are beneficial, such as feelings of happiness, prosperity or optimism. However, if you make deposits of self-doubt, despair or hopelessness, your mental bank is going to go into financial crisis and default on you!

If you control the deposits into your "subconscious bank," why not make those deposits the best they can be? Would you rather deposit copper in your bank or pure platinum?

Here's the best part! Your bank accepts **everything that is deposited!**

Even if it isn't real in your conscious state.

Let me say that again: Your subconscious is going to accept what you feed it as being real.

So, when you use visualization to see your goals and outcomes as already being achieved and successful, you will start to unconsciously do the things, be in the places, meet the people, and take on the challenges that will transform your subconscious thoughts into your physical reality.

Remember when I told you about Michael Phelps and the visualization techniques that he used every single day during his training. This is exactly it!

Let's get a better understand regarding the history of visualization and some of the earliest 20th century pioneers who helped bring it to the mainstream.

The 20th century history of visualization

It is not a new concept at all, in fact, it has been written about for centuries but started gaining ground in the early 20th century. It's important to recognize the lives and works of three great authors at that time, helping pave the way for our current foundation of visualization to be laid:

Wallace Wattles, Charles F. Haanel, and Napoleon Hill.

In 1910, Wallace Wattles published, "The Science of Getting Rich," which was later followed by the works of Charles F. Haanel with his 1916 book, "The Master Key System." And if both of these authors are not familiar to you, their works helped paved the way for the teachings of Napoleon Hill and his own works, "Think and Grow Rich."

If you remember the book that came out in 2006, "The Secret," by Rhonda Byrne, Wattles' book was a major source of inspiration for her writing it.

Before diving deep into visualization, understanding the works of these authors will provide you with a better appreciation of its importance, helping guide you during the process.

Wallace Wattles' premise was that the universe is an unlimited formless "substance" that is just waiting for us, or anyone else, to transform it into a **material being**. The main theme of this material being was generating financial wealth, because he was of the belief that seeking riches was the key to helping provide value to many more people. There are several other main concepts that I wish to press upon you, which will help build your foundation for visualization as well.

This formless "substance" could be used by anyone and everyone, thus, it rules out the concept that there is only but so much abundance and wealth to go around. If you visualized what you desired over and over, in time, your desires would be a physical manifestation of the substance.

However, there are three prerequisites that Wallace mentioned for your creation to reach its maximum potential:

1. Being in harmony with the universe

2. Having a mindset of creation and not competition with others

3. Expressing gratitude

Fortunately, these are all concepts that you have expanded upon before!

When you are in harmony with the universe, you are maximizing your efforts to become the best version of yourself. It all goes back to the core values that you identified earlier. Being in alignment, in harmony, with the core values that define you, places you in a unique position to be a positive influence upon others, whether you realize it or not. As Wallace says, "God made you to make the most of yourself, which in turn, makes you more valuable to others."

When you have a mindset of creation and not competition with others, it helps eliminate the pattern or preconception that "there is not enough to go around." Think of abundance as an unlimited source, ready to be tapped into. Because this abundance exists, there is no need to compete for it with others. Believe that there are no obstacles, other than yourself, that will stop you from visualizing and creating the life that your desire. Your goals may be lofty and challenging; however, they are attainable because the substance that will create them has unlimited possibilities and pathways for you to achieve them. So, if you feel that time, money, or understanding are roadblocks towards your success, know this, visualizing and creating the reality that you want is entirely within you!

Finally, having gratitude for what you already have is key. I previously talked about the power of gratitude and the impact that is has upon our lives. Once you are harmonious with the substance, appreciating what it has created for you now, it will naturally gravitate towards the newly visualized things—your goals and outcomes, which you desire.

In 1912, Charles Haanel published his works, first as a correspondence course over 24 weeks then as a book, "The Master Key System." Among the many amazing topics that it focused on, it included powerful descriptions and exercises regarding the Law of Attraction and creative visualization.

Mr. Haanel's book included powerful visualization techniques that were built up in sequences, allowing people to see, hear, and feel in various situations. This is what we're going to be practicing as we move further along in this trimester.

In his teachings, he discussed a critical step towards getting the things that you desire in life. You must have a clear picture of what you desire combined with a positive mindset that you have the confidence that this desire will be achieved. It's not about hoping that you will get what you desire in your life, it's about knowing with absolute certainty that what you desire in life will come to be.

He further reinforced this absolute desire and level of confidence with visualization techniques of creating and having a mental picture of exactly what you desire. Breaking it down into various steps such as visualizing a familiar place, remembering the details of a photograph such as their smile, visible emotions, and facial features are the initial steps to practice learning how to visualize and recall images with an increasing level of clarity. This was followed by more complex visualization techniques, where he had you visualize a construction of an entire battleship, further honing your skills and power of being able to visualize complex situations in multiple timelines.

It's going to be a similar process on how I will guide you through your own visualization techniques later in the chapter.

Finally, there are the works of Napoleon Hill, author of the book, "Think and Grow Rich." One of the techniques that elevated his success was the development of the visualization technique called the "invisible counselors." It was so controversial at the time that Mr. Hill originally thought of not including it within the works.

The way I like to think of the "invisible counselors" technique is like visualization on steroids!

This is beyond simple visualization where you are seeing, hearing, and feeling different pictures, sounds, and internal feeling. This is about creating a mastermind group that is highly interactive. Napoleon Hill's group of invisible counselors included such people as Socrates, Aristotle, Abraham Lincoln, Thomas Edison, and Isaac Newton. He would have vivid and creative conversations with them, providing him inspiration, wisdom, guidance, and counseling. It didn't matter if the people that he used were alive or dead, or if they were total strangers that he had never met. He harnessed the power of his subconscious to visualize intricate conversations and interactions that he credits with some of his more profound ideas and works.

The powerful aspect of this technique is that it is only limited by your level of creativity. Now you may feel that you are not the most creative person. I'm confident that as you progress through practicing visualization, you will get to the level where anything that you wish to imagine is within the realm of your possibility!

As you continue to flow through this third trimester, I am going to break things down on a physiological level and help you understand exactly how the brain works. This is going to be key for optimizing the visualization techniques that you will soon begin to practice.

How the brain works

It's important to have a quick science lesson on how your brain patterns work. The brain is much more powerful than you realize so let's harness its untapped energy!

There are four main types of brainwaves that exist (actually five but let's keep it simple):

1. Beta waves, "Our Conscious Sate"

2. Alpha waves, "Our Deeper Relaxed State"

3. Theta waves, "Our Meditative and Light Sleeping State"

4. Delta waves, "Our Deep Sleep State"

They are listed in this order because we are starting with a state of full consciousness (Beta) all the way towards full unconsciousness (Delta).

Beta waves are the fastest cycling waves present during your conscious state. They facilitate conscious endeavors and daily tasks such as decision making, being alert or utilizing any mental activity.

As you drift more towards unconsciousness, your brainwaves slow down and transition into **Alpha waves**.

When you physically and mentally slow down, the Alpha waves take over. You are still in a conscious state but think of it as being somewhat drowsy. You are aware of what's going on around you but have that heightened energy or alertness.

Your visualization exercises will get your brain in a state of producing Alpha waves.

Next, continuing the slowdown of your brainwaves, you develop **Theta waves**. At this point, you will have slipped into a state of lessened consciousness and light sleep (close but not fully asleep yet!). Dream formation will begin to occur here and is associated with REM sleep or rapid eye movement.

Finally, your deep sleep begins and there is total loss of your surroundings and your brainwaves are at their slowest. This state is dominated by **Delta waves**. It represents your subconscious state and is important to reach each night because of its regenerative powers, both physically and mentally.

Again, what's the importance of the Alpha waves? Well, when we get your brain towards an Alpha wave state, you will remain conscious yet be in a relaxed state that will facilitate the visualization techniques that I will go over shortly!

Think of the Alpha state as the bridge between your conscious (Beta) state and subconscious (Theta) state.

In short, when you visualize, you are creating brand new neural pathways. Your neural pathways are the roadmaps of your mind, creating your learned behaviors and memories. Once these mental pathways are created, it facilitates the physical actions that will help you obtain your goals and outcomes.

Visualization is going to further develop and enhance the **right side** of your brain. The left side, or hemisphere, of your brain is typically known as your **logic center**. Within the left hemisphere of your brain, you can:

Make logical decisions

Work mathematical and scientific problems

Use your language abilities or speak

The **right side**, or hemisphere, of your brain is typically known as your **creative center**. Within the right hemisphere of your brain, you can:

Express emotions

Be creative and imaginative

Develop intuition

What happens as you learn how to enhance the right side of your brain through visualization?

You will start to make that shift from thinking of things in a logical manner to becoming more creative. You will begin to access the creative and emotional being within you, maximizing all your emotions and senses. As you continue to practice, it will become more than just "seeing" how things look for you, it will be an experience of all five senses.

I remember many years ago when I was doing my pilot lessons, going through my preflight check lists. All pilots, well at least any sane pilot, will go through these to make sure everything is safe and secure BEFORE taking off.

I remember walking around the outside of the plane, checking all the surface areas, making sure the cables were properly connected. Checking the propeller to make sure there were no splits or cracks within it. Inside, I would check my gauges, making sure they were all functional, checking the fluid levels (most importantly the amount of fuel!), check the function of the control surfaces and on and on.

The preflight check is the foundation for operating a plane safely like your core values are the foundation for operating your life safely. Hopping in a plane without doing your checks and finding out you have an oil pressure problem 4000 feet up can be a challenging place to be!

Now, here is the really cool part of visualization. As I overcame my fear of flying, I realized that I was visualizing the flight in advance and that was key towards having a more comfortable, safe, and most importantly, fun flight!

I would pause for a minute or two in the cockpit before starting the engines and use a variety of emotions and senses.

I felt the wind coming in from the opened side windows, feeling how refreshing and cool it was.

I saw the beauty of the surface of the earth, with its fields and buildings and structures, lined up like a fun jigsaw puzzle.

I heard the low hum of the engine as we slowed down the plane.

I could smell the fresh air 4000 feet up, free from the smog of the cars.

I felt excitement as I climbed higher in the air and expressed joy as I was able to overcome my long-term fears.

There was a funny thing that happened four months into my training. I was with my instructor, practicing my turns and maneuvers. He calmly asked me, yet in a serious voice, "Terence, what's wrong?"

I started immediately looking over my instruments again, making sure that everything was correct. Looking outside the window, there was no traffic in my area and I was on course.

I said "Jeff, I don't see the problem." After he finished laughing out loud, I asked him again, with a little more determination in my voice, "Jeff, what is wrong?"

He simply stated, "Remember when you did your first flight you wanted to jump out of the plane because of all of the shaking? You're not doing that now. Today, you are relaxed and calm"

I finally realized that we were in the middle of very windy conditions. The plane was shaking all over the place. In the past, I would have freaked out and panicked. But this time was different.

I wasn't scared!

Not only did it not bother me, I didn't even realize how bad the plane was shaking. I shifted my mindset from the anxiety and analytical components of my left brain towards the emotional and creative aspects of my right. I was simply having fun and experiencing the senses of the experience.

That's the power of visualization!

Understanding what you visualize now

I am going to teach you how to tap into your senses and emotions, creating a realistic picture of how life looks the way that you desire. It will be a picture so real and vivid that your mind accepts it as reality.

This is why top athletes love visualization because studies have shown that as athletes add visualization techniques to their physical routines, it enhances them on a physical level, whether it be strength, speed, or endurance.

It's the exact technique that I used when sitting in my car before my third triathlon race, having a panic attack about swimming in the water. I saw myself mentally swimming the perfect race, without fear or doubt. After I visualized the perfect race and physically hit the water, it became my reality.

Now, this didn't just happen overnight!

I didn't just turn superhuman in a matter of minutes and swim that race. I was practicing visualization for **months before this**. Repetition helped develop the necessary neural pathways, which was just as effective at swimming as the physical event itself.

You can, and you will use your thoughts to create your own neural pathways for success.

What are you visualizing now?

You visualize all the time either through your dreams or daydreams. It happens all the time. The question I have for you is this?

What are you visualizing now? Are you visualizing success in your life or having intermittent visions of failure?

We all have room for growth and that's what you're going to tap into right now. Because we are not perfect beings, you are bound to have both positive and negative visualizations about your life.

It is very challenging to have thoughts that are positive 100% of the time. Your goal is to have positive visualizations more often than not.

Remember the Law of Attraction?

The Law of Attraction states that whatever you put your attention to can and will become your reality. In order to optimize your chances for success, you must focus your attention towards the thoughts, events and actions in your life that will either improve or enhance it. So, if you have core values of feeling joyful or confident, your positive thoughts will attract the things that you desire.

Understand that The Law of Attraction is a neutral entity. It has no bias towards the positive and the negative. You can equally attract negative events towards your life as easily as you attract the positive ones. So, having thoughts of not feeling smart, being miserable at work, or not having the relationship that you desire will attract the things in your life that will reinforce this.

Do you continually reflect upon things in your life that you may not have been so successful with in the past or currently not successful with now? They could be things such as your current employment or your family or your financial situation.

Are you visualizing yourself in a negative way?

Do you wake up in the morning and some of your first thoughts are that you have another eight to 10 hours of grueling work at the office? Are you watching the clock on Friday afternoon, anxious to get out of the workplace and have the weekend off because it's been a long and frustrating week?

Do you have visions of not wanting to come home after work because you can just "see" yourself getting into another argument or not even communicating it all?

Do you look at the mail on the kitchen counter, having visual thoughts of seeing yourself not being able to get out from under your pile of bills?

The sad thing is many people don't even realize that they are doing this, continuing to attract that negative energy towards them. They wonder why there's no significant change in their lives.

The good thing is that you will begin to start the process of visualizing the things that are going to move your life forward in a more productive way. With a little practice and focus, you will do it!

Still, you may tell yourself, "Even if I begin to visualize events in a more positive way it doesn't change the situation that I'm in right now."

It does change the situation now. It's all about the mindset that you have and how you visualize things in a different way. For example, when looking at that pile of mail on the kitchen counter, instead of visualizing your finances in a negative way you can look at it differently. You could have visions that you are grateful for having these bills because they wouldn't be there if you didn't have a home to live in. When going to work first thing in the morning or itching to run out on a Friday afternoon, instead of visualizing the negative aspects of your job, see it in a positive way. Visualize that you are appreciative and grateful for even having a job and income in the first place, unlike millions of people in the world.

Visualization is all about your mindset and you have the power to create your reality. And if you have the power to create your own reality, wouldn't it serve you to have a positive visualization that works in your favor?

The benefits that you gain from visualization

Let's address three things that you can gain from learning visualization, which are:

1. Developing your mental roadmap

2. Gaining mentally and physically

3. Becoming a kid again!

The mental roadmap

Visualizing is a process that is crucial for jumpstarting your journey towards getting the goals and outcomes that you desire. It is one of the two components that the super successful do, the other one being taking action.

If you can't **see** yourself in advance reaching the goal or at least reaching the intermediate steps towards that goal, then how likely do you feel that you will be successful?

When you visualize, you are mentally laying down the pathway from the person that you are now towards the goals and outcomes that you will achieve. In time, this will help with your transformation towards the outcome that you desire. Without having a picture of that mental roadmap preset in your mind, the path becomes fuzzy, unclear and then suddenly, fear sneaks in. You lack a picture of success to fall back on when the doubts begin to creep in because you haven't created it.

Using repetitive techniques of visualization creates a stacking effect. The more you do it, the more you see yourself achieving your desired goals and outcomes. That is powerful, especially if you start from a place of fear or apprehension. Having the visual picture slowly builds the confidence that will be needed to get you towards the end.

As I discussed before in the module of fear, you will overcome fear by acting first and building the confidence later. **This is the "confidence later" portion.** Visualization is the portion that reinforces the action that you just took, empowering you to see a successful future you. This in turn drives you towards taking more action. It's a mental loop that gets stronger with each action and visualization.

Your mental roadmap does not just contain the start and finish lines.

It is a journey.

Anywhere along the path, you can use visualization to bring you closer towards success. Don't just focus on the end result. You have the power to focus on any waypoint along the way, which can be more optimal for you. For some, they may not be able to mentally see or believe the end point when they initially start. However, they can be more successful in seeing a waypoint along the path to success. Visualizing your success in small pieces will make the journey easier for you!

Say, for example, you have a goal of wanting to speak in front of an audience of 100 people because your outcome is to become a more confident person. Now, if you have a fear of speaking and have never given speeches in front of more than 10 people, this may be daunting. If you try to visualize yourself speaking to the group of 100, you still may have some underlying fears and doubts about doing it.

Your subconscious is like a bank that accepts whatever you deposit within it. If you deposit the picture of speaking to 100 people, your subconscious may not accept it because you are most likely holding onto the fear associated with such a large group.

So, what do you do in a case like this, a time when you can't 100% OWN your goal and outcomes with confidence?

Make a smaller deposit in your bank until you are ready to make the big one!

In this case, visualize yourself speaking to 15-20 people which might not be a stretch for you since you have done it in front of 10.

The numbers don't matter.

The point is to visualize smaller waypoints along the way and develop the neural pathways that will develop the physical attributes that you desire.

Mental and physical gains

Visualization goes far beyond your achievement of goals and outcomes. Probably one of the biggest benefits of it is the physical and mental relaxation that it provides.

When you are operating day to day, remember, your brain is kicking out Beta waves, actively moving you through the day. But at the same time, a lot of mental and physical energy and exertion comes, increasing levels of stress and anxiety.

Give your brain a break!

Slipping into two or three sessions of Alpha wave execution slows your brain down, getting you more relaxed and calmer. Blood pressure, pulse rate, and breathing are all slowed down, physically helping to overcome the stress that you may have built up from you being in a prolonged Beta state.

Imagine having a technique that will relax you when you feel stressed or overwhelmed. Being able to put your body and mind into a relaxed state will not only improve you physically but mentally.

As the physical manifestations of stress and anxiety diminish, you gain enhanced mental clarity. When your brain slows down and eliminates the toxic clutter that filled it, your enhanced clarity will allow you to be more creative. You gain more ability to "think outside the box," having higher levels of creativity and the ability to solve any problems or issues more efficiently.

Becoming a kid again!

The younger kids are, the less exposure they have to the patterns of influence that are imprinted within their subconscious.

When we are born, we only have TWO fears:

The fear of falling and the fear of loud noises.

That's it.

As we get older two critical things happen:

The first is that we get imprinted with the values that are placed upon us by family, friends, teachers, and society. We may be told, "Don't talk back to your elders," or "Money is the root of all evil," or the cookie cutter statement: "Go to school, get a job, and work hard for 30 years then retire."

Second, we lose our creativity and powers of visualization.

Do you remember yourself or a close friend having an "imaginary friend?"

What ever happened to him or her? Well, they slowly dissipated away because likely, there was an adult who told you or them that they shouldn't imagine "fake" things and just to stick with reality.

Visualization brings back the kid in us because it opens our mind to create anything that we desire. The only limitation is your imagination! You will learn to reopen that creativity that you had and may have lost so many years ago.

And as we go back towards becoming kids again and visualize, we start to get back our invincibility.

Remember when you were a kid and did things back in the day that you would NEVER let your kids do today? Remember the bumps and bruises because you did and tried things without fear?

That's the mindset that visualization will provide, allowing you to see yourself as successful in the goals and outcomes that you desire. Seeing yourself as fearless, with a slight touch of invincibility that anything and everything is within your grasp!

Revisiting your outcomes

In the first trimester of the circle of life, you've built the foundation by describing your life broken down into three main outcomes, which were:

1. Your personal self

2. Your social self

3. Your financial self

So, the next step is to create and write down one outcome that you personally would like to achieve in each one of these "selves."

You are ahead of the game if you took the time to do the exercise in Chapter 7, called "Develop Your Outcomes," because you drafted three outcomes for each one of your "selves." You can go back to:

https://www.docdeliversbooks.com/free-ebook/

to download the worksheet again.

Don't worry if your outcomes may be unclear at this time. Understand that these outcomes don't have to be the final ones that you **ACT** upon during your **REBIRTH** section. We are just using these as a template to help guide you with the visualization techniques that are coming up shortly.

So, for this exercise, select one outcome from each of the three categories.

If you are still unclear or uncertain about the outcomes that you desire, I will provide you with examples of each one of them.

Your personal self includes the categories of feelings, fitness, and fun. Outcomes that you can design within this category include examples such as:

Having an outcome to overcome your shyness by talking to two new people each week for the next four weeks.

Having an outcome to lose 20 pounds in the next 90 days.

Having an outcome to have a fun and exciting day trip once per month for the next three months.

Your external self includes the categories of family, faith, and following. Some outcomes that you may have regarding this could be:

Having an outcome to have a family outing out of town once per month.

Having an outcome to spend 10 minutes every day for 30 days reading a spiritual body of work.

Having an outcome to share a positive message three times a week for the next month on Facebook live.

Your financial self includes the categories of your internal financial worth, your external financial value, and your core financial happiness, which includes examples of outcomes such as:

Having an outcome to grow your business by 10% in the next 90 days.

Having an outcome to provide volunteer services in a homeless shelter for a total of eight hours in the next 30 days.

Having an outcome to design an office plan that will improve the morale of your fellow coworkers within the next 90 days.

Now, even though I provided you with several example of outcomes, I really encourage you to choose outcomes that you desire in your life. They are likely to be more congruent with the newly developed core values that you have established during your first trimester. Take the time to write down your outcomes in each of the categories. It doesn't have to be perfect because the wording of your outcomes is really going to get more specific in the next section within the Circle of Conception called ACT. For now, let's work with the first thing that comes to mind so that you will have a platform to practice your visualization techniques.

With your three outcomes written down, I want you to put these to the side for now. You are not going to start practicing visualization with these outcomes just yet. Like the model that Charles Haanel used, you're going to start the process of visualization in building blocks, using situations that you are already comfortable and familiar with, eventually building towards the more complex visualization techniques like Napoleon Hill's "Invisible Counselors" visualization technique.

Revisiting your core values

The second component that you will use for the upcoming visualization techniques will be your core values, which were also developed in your first trimester within your Circle of Conception. Are you beginning to see a pattern how your flow in development through the first trimester is providing the building blocks that are continuing to enhance and move your life towards the outcomes that you desire?

Reflect upon the three to five core values that you previously established. You will use them with the outcomes that you have created. In the first trimester, you created your core values based on the person that you wished to *BE*. Now as you continue to flow through this third trimester in your circle of life, you are going to start to visualize and *SEE* yourself as the person that you wish to be.

If needed, you can download the worksheets for your core values at:

https://www.docdeliversbooks.com/free-ebook/

and scroll down to the section called "Core Values."

Pay attention because this is a critical step prior to getting to the next phase of your Circle of Conception which is you beginning to *ACT*, moving towards the goals and outcomes that you desire in the future. And as you are moving towards your future self with the core values that will represent the newly delivered and enhanced version of yourself, you are going to learn how to SEE yourself as a future version of you right now. Your subconscious cannot determine the difference between what is real and what is not. Wouldn't it serve you to see yourself as a more confident person now, even though that may not be the person that you are today? It's like you are taking a snapshot with a special futuristic camera that is taking pictures of the person that you wish to be in the future. You are holding a future picture in your hand right now and visualizing yourself today as the person that's in your photograph.

Put your core values and your three outcomes you have written down to the side at this time and let's start the fun process of building the techniques to help you visualize!

Basics of visualization and building the blocks

One of the most exciting times during a woman's pregnancy is when she and the family have either that first ultrasound in the first trimester or they had that second trimester ultrasound that shows them the sex of the baby. In my experience, I've seen a lot more joy in smiles and women's faces after they witness the second ultrasound! In today's world, we not only have 3-D ultrasound, but we have four-dimensional ultrasound that provides an amazing snapshot of the unborn child. Many times, with the snapshot, I hear women talk about future features about their babies such as their smile or dimples or hair, seeing the picture of the future version of their child that physically doesn't exist in that moment in time. Like a 4-D ultrasound, you're going to start the process of starting with a tangible and realistic picture that you see now and will expand upon in various steps. These steps are going to help you practice visualization and slowly build the blocks that will enhance it.

Unlike the time-tested 3-D ultrasound that is used to provide a quick snapshot of your reality now, you are going to develop your mindset at the quality level of the 4-D ultrasound.

It's time to see the future version of yourself right now!

It's an exciting prospect because you're going to tap into your creativity to see things more vividly than you otherwise may do on your own. As I stated before, the only limitation in your ability to visualize is your level of creativity. No matter how out-of-the-box or unrealistic your visualization may be, humor me for a while throughout the rest of this chapter and practice the techniques that I will present to you.

Building blocks of visualization

As you start this process of visualization right now, the first thing that I require of you is that you are in a quiet setting with no distractions and you are seated in a comfortable and relaxed position.

The second thing that I require of you is to treat this as a building block process. If you haven't practiced visualization techniques in the past, you are going to want to pace yourself. You may find yourself getting frustrated initially because your vision may not have the clarity that you desire. The last thing I want you to do is to quit the process.

Third, because these are building blocks, take a moment to reflect and practice each specific building block before moving to the next one. That doesn't mean that you must master each building block and have a perfect visualization before moving to the next one. I just don't want you to power through this section and encompass all the building blocks at once. Remember, this level is "focus" and here you are focusing on understanding each building block slowly, not fast-tracking it!

So, are you in a quiet setting where you are relaxed and comfortable?

Do you commit to not quitting and continuing to practice the visualization techniques, even if you find it hard and challenging in the beginning?

Can you make the promise not to rush through the techniques of visualization, absorbing each one in a relaxed pace?

With that being said, you are going to have fun and bring out the inner child in you as you start to get creative with visualization and have fun with the process!

Let's get started!

Building Block 1: Seeing a Familiar Scenario

The next four building blocks will gradually build your ability to effectively visualize. Each building block contains two components:

The Breathing and Tension Releasing component (uniform among all four blocks)

The Building Block component (specific to the exercise)

I have put together a worksheet that you can download to get the script for the each of the components. Reading and recording your voice would be ideal as you listen to the script. However, simply reading from the book or the downloaded worksheet will work as well.

You can access the Breathing and Tension and four separate building blocks by going to:

https://www.docdeliversbooks.com/free-ebook/

and scroll down to the section called "Tension Release, Breathing and Visualization Building Blocks."

At this point, you either should be sitting or working your way toward sitting, in a quiet environment and comfortable position.

Imagine all the tension leaving your body as it falls away from you. Let gravity do its work and imagine your head and neck relaxed, feeling limp, and without any tension. And, as this slowly falls away, the tension that is leaving your body moves towards your shoulders and your upper back. The pockets of tension bind like two raindrops that merge together, and they get even bigger and start to fall away even faster. The tension is now rolling down your back and you feel the tension moving away out of your hips as you feel yourself in your upper body totally relaxed, sinking more into the comfortable position that you're already in. This giant raindrop of tension continues to flow down your thighs and moves towards your knees and now you're feeling your feet start to sink further into the floor as the tension migrates to your feet and slowly flows away from your body like water that is going down the side of a hill.

Next you are going to take three deep breaths starting with the first breath, breathe in three seconds then breathe out. As you breathe out, feel any residual tension exhaling from your body. Breathe in again, collecting the last residual tension, and breathe out. One more time, take a deep breath in and the last of your tension is slowly exhaled away and you feel totally relaxed and at ease. Now I want you to focus on your inner thoughts.

Visualization scenario 1

See yourself walking down a white hallway that has no sounds or colors and as you continue to walk down this hallway you come upon a white door. On this white door is a red doorknob and you see yourself reaching your hand out slowly turning the red doorknob and pushing the door wide open. After the doors open you see a big white room that is totally quiet and empty. This room is huge, and you don't see any walls at all. And now, you're going to begin to imagine that this is one of the rooms in your own home that you are currently not sitting in right now. The walls begin to form in this big white room and the room is slowly starting to shrink to the size of your own bedroom in your home. Start to add the pieces of furniture to this empty white room positioning each piece of furniture exactly as it is in your own home. Now, you start adding color to the walls and the colors are slowly starting to match those same colors that are within your bedroom.

Now, with all the furniture in the room and the colors on the walls, you begin to walk into your bedroom and start looking around. As you take each step, listen to your footsteps as you start to walk about your room. Pay attention to the sounds they make, no matter how subtle they may seem. You start to touch the pieces of furniture and they feel exactly as they do in your own room; some pieces may feel soft like the bed while others may feel hard like a nightstand or table.

Walk around your bedroom and start to see more detail within any items of furniture that are around. Imagine the colors starting to get slightly more intensified and vivid. Now imagine yourself getting in your bed on top of all the covers and sheets and continuing to feel relaxed staring upwards at the ceiling. Start looking at the color of your sheets that are on your bed and start to feel the texture of them as they are touching the back of your head and extremities. You begin to roll around on your bed from edge to edge, hearing the sounds that the bed is making.

Now, it's time to get out of your bed and imagine your bare feet hitting the floor, feeling the texture of the surface and the temperature of the floor beneath the soles of your feet. Looking down at the floor, you start to notice its color and pattern, and you stare at the floor as you stand up from the bed and slowly walk around it back and forth. You take another look at the doorway to your bedroom and before you walk out you take one final look at all the furniture around the bedroom. You see all the items in clear detail and you can see all the colors of each particular item.

You slowly walked towards the bedroom door and as you exit the bedroom you grab the red handle of the door and you slowly close it. You are now back in the white hallway and now you begin to direct your focus back towards where you are sitting right now, slowly becoming more aware of your situation, where you are, and if your eyes are closed you open them. You start to look around the room and begin to realize you are back in the place where you started.

How did you do?

Were you able to feel calm and relaxed before you even started the process of visualization, feeling the tension leaving your body and feeling the peace in that moment?

This building block on visualization focused on you starting to practice visualizing with a scenario that you're already familiar with, which was your bedroom. Were you able to recall the pieces of furniture and items within your room? Were you able to see the colors of the walls and the pieces of furniture in some detail? Did you have the sensations of feeling the texture of your sheets on your bed or the feeling of the floor beneath your bare feet?

If not, what was challenging for you to recall? You still did an excellent job because you took the initiative to even do this exercise in the first place! So, congratulate yourself for your success no matter what your visual outcome was. It takes time to get to a point where visualization will create images in your mind that are vivid and as detailed as if you were physically looking at it yourself, but that time will come for you.

During this building block you focused on three aspects of your senses. Your visual, your auditory, and your kinesthetic or feeling. You didn't really focus on the other two senses such as smell and taste because to do that I would've had to figure out a creative way to stick a portion of your kitchen and eating area within your bedroom! For now, understand that your visual, auditory, and kinesthetic sensors are going to be your three most powerful senses that you will use in visualization. Also realize that with you starting this process, I do not want to overwhelm you with visualizing all five of your senses.

Practice doing this a few times each day and when you feel more comfortable with creating the sights, sounds, and feel of your bedroom, you're going to add the second building block which encompasses your emotions.

Before moving to the next section, make sure that you feel comfortable with your ability to do the basics of visualization because you are going to begin the slow transition to a place that may not be as familiar to you.

Building Block 2: Adding Emotions to Your Visual Picture and Enhancing the Scene

The next step in the building block is starting to add an emotional state to the picture. You are going to start to feel the emotions that are associated within the environment that you create in your mind. While you are doing this, you will continue to see the picture as vividly as possible, taking in all the sights, sounds, and feelings of your specific scenario.

Now, you're going to enhance your senses by playing around with sizes and intensity. You did a little bit of it in the last building block with trying to enhance the vividness of the colors but you're going to take that one step further with all three of the senses that you practiced before.

Again, make sure you're in a comfortable place where you are sitting without any distractions because you're about to start the second building block for your visualization.

Visualization scenario 2

Imagine all the tension leaving your body as it falls away from you. Let gravity do its work and imagine your head and neck relaxed, feeling limp and without any tension. And, as this slowly falls away, the tension that is leaving your body moves towards your shoulders and your upper back. The pockets of tension bind like two raindrops that merge together and get even bigger and start to fall away even faster. The tension is now rolling down your back and you feel the tension moving away out of your hips as you feel yourself in your upper body totally relaxed, sinking more into the comfortable position that you're already in. This giant raindrop of tension continues to flow down your thighs and moves towards your knees and now you're feeling your feet start to sink further into the floor as the tension migrates to your feet and slowly flows away from your body like water that is going down the side of a hill.

Next, you are going to take three deep breaths starting with the first breath, breathe in three seconds then breathe out and as you breathe out, feel any residual tension exhaling from your body. Breathe in again, collecting out last residual tension, and breathe out. One more time, take a deep breath in and the last of your tension is slowly exhaled away and you feel totally relaxed and at ease. Now, I want you to focus on your inner thoughts and start to see your surroundings slowly getting blurrier and fading away.

See yourself walking down a white hallway that has no sounds or colors and as you continue to walk down this hallway you come upon a white door. On this white door is a red doorknob and you see yourself reaching your hand out slowly turning the red doorknob and pushing the door wide open. After the doors open, you see an empty beach before your eyes on a bright and sunny day.

You take four steps out of the hallway and now you are standing on the beach with its clean, white, and warm sand beneath the soles of your feet. You slowly hear a creaking sound and you gently turn your head to the side and see the door with the red knob slowly closing. As the door closes shut you hear a slight clicking sound, the doorway itself disappearing. You turn your head back towards the white sand and clear blue ocean in front of you. As you start to take steps towards the water, you feel the warmth of the sandy beach and you begin to feel the warmth of the bright sun on your skin. It feels so pleasant and you have the sensation of feeling so relaxed and at peace at this moment in time.

You're the only one on the beach because it is your beach and no one else's, and you feel excited about being able to have fun and enjoy yourself on the beach without any distractions or worries. You start walking faster towards the ocean and begin to start a light run in anticipation of hitting the cool water. Now, you hear yourself laugh as the inner child within you gets ever so closer to the water that you are now running to. You're not the only one laughing as you hear the sound of seagulls above you and as you look up and shield your eyes from the bright sun, you start to see the seagulls circling around in a playful manner, making a sound that almost sounds like they are laughing with you and enjoying themselves as well.

Your feet finally hit the cool water and you feel that instant transition from the warm sand to the cold yet relaxing water that is swirling around your ankles. You stop running and as you see the blue gentle waves slowly coming in, each one hits your ankles with a wave of coolness that makes you so giddy and excited to have your time here. Now you look at the sun and you feel its warmth on your face. You reach out towards it with your right hand and imagine yourself grasping the sun, slowly turning it clockwise to diminish its brightness. You feel yourself becoming a little bit cooler right now, but it's still comfortable. You decrease the brightness of the sun to the point where you can stare at it directly without any discomfort or worry.

You walk a little further into the water and now you are waist-high looking down at the clear blue water beneath you. As you look in the water you begin to see small goldfish gently swimming around you in a circular pattern. As these goldfish are swimming around, you start to see them getting bigger in size, growing from the size of your pinky to the size of your hand. You reach into the water and you can feel their rough scales gently brushing across the back of your hands as they swim by. And as they continue to swim you start to see the fish's golden colors get even brighter. Your excitement rises, and you begin to laugh.

Now, they look like shining stars underneath the water. You slowly turn around, walking back towards the shore. As you hit the sand you feel that instant transition from the coolness of the water to the warmth of the sand. You're feeling a little chilly from the water, so you look back at the sun as you're standing on the beach and you turn the sun like that red doorknob that brought you here in the first place and gently rotate it to increase its warmth and intensity. You feel warm, calm, and at peace.

As you walk back up the beach towards the place where you first started you see one of the goldfish hovering in the air and it begins to get larger and larger, slowly shifting its shape into the white doorway that you first entered. Now you look at the doorknob and it's a bright, shining, golden color and before you grab it you take one more look at the beach and remember how much fun you had on this day. You hear yourself laughing, knowing that this is not the end and you will be back here shortly.

You look back at the gold doorknob and gently turn it, the door opening outward towards the clear white hallway that you started with. As you step into the doorway, slowly hearing its creaking sound again, you look at the last bits of the beach and the ocean before the door closes completely and you hear it lock. Now you begin to direct your focus back towards where you are sitting right now and slowly become more aware of your situation. You start to look around the room and begin to realize you are back in the place where you started.

How did you do?

Did you get better at visualizing the different sights, sounds, and feelings in this scenario at the beach? And ask yourself what your emotional state was while you were visualizing. Were you able to feel yourself feeling happy, joyful, and at peace? Did you internally experience joy as you were laughing and running towards the water? How did your play go with altering the sensations of the warmth of the sun and the size and color of the fish in the water?

Again, continue to practice these techniques because the more that you do them daily the more vivid and detailed the images will become for you.

Building Block 3: Seeing Yourself Express Your Core Values

After completing and practicing the first two building blocks, you now have a firm foundation of the basics of visualization. I encourage you to practice your visualization techniques twice a day, once in the morning and once in the evening or however your time permits. The key to getting good at visualization, or anything else in life, is repetitive practice. You may be crappy at it right now, however, if you commit to doing this twice a day, you're going to realize that in 60 days your visualizations will be so vivid and clear. It's as if you're looking at the picture with your own eyes.

So now it's time to step it up a notch and practice visualization incorporating your core values. Recall one of the three to five core values that define you. You are going to imagine yourself in a place or situation where you are fully expressing this core value. For example, you may have a core value of confidence and you can picture yourself giving a speech confidently to hundreds of people at a seminar. Or you can have a core value such as commitment, seeing yourself being on time for your appointments and meetings, keeping up with the commitments that you made to yourself and others.

As I guide you through this script, understand that it's going to be a generalized guidance because you already have the tools to visualize what you see, feel, or hear along with the tools to add emotions that you can feel and express. One of the things that has really helped me with my visualization tools is to write out a visualization that I would like for myself. Then I record it on my phone so that I always have it with me when I need it. So, I simplify the process by pulling out my phone and listening to my visualization script that is specifically written for me. This building block will provide you the basics of how you should talk yourself through visualization of your core values, and later I encourage you to create your own script that is more specific towards the core value that you wish to express.

In this building block, you will continue to add on the previous components that you've already established and practiced. Within this building block you're going to add outside people and/or situations to make the visualization more realistic. That's why we started with you all alone on the beach, to simplify the process but now you are ready to add a little bit more complexity to your visualization.

I know you can do it!

The second component that you will add to this specific building block is seeing yourself from the third person. Shortly, you will begin seeing the world through your eyes, expressing your core values. Seeing, feeling, and hearing yourself within your situation while simultaneously expressing and feeling your emotions. And as you progress through the visualization that I will take you through, you will begin to see yourself as an observer doing all these actions as if you are watching a movie of yourself.

For this visualization, since it's specific to your core value that you selected, you're going to have to determine a place, time, or situation where you are fully expressing that core value. The purpose for the script is to help guide and augment your senses, emotions, and feelings within the environment that you've created for yourself, adding additional people to make it more realistic and then practicing seeing yourself from the third person.

Have you selected the situation or environment that you wish to play in?

Excellent!

As always, you want to get in a comfortable place that is free of distractions and quiet, so that we may begin!

Visualization scenario 3

Imagine all the tension leaving your body as it falls away from you. Let gravity do its work and imagine your head and neck relaxed, feeling limp and without any tension. And, as this slowly falls away, the tension that is leaving your body moves towards your shoulders and your upper back. The pockets of tension bind like two raindrops that merge together and get even bigger and start to fall away even faster. The tension is now rolling down your back and you feel the tension moving away out of your hips as you feel yourself in your upper body totally relaxed, sinking more into the comfortable position that you're already in. This giant raindrop of tension continues to flow down your thighs and moves towards your knees and now you're feeling your feet start to sink further into the floor as the tension migrates to your feet and slowly flows away from your body like water that is going down the side of a hill.

Next, you are going to take three deep breaths starting with the first breath, breathe in three seconds then breathe out and as you breathe out feel any residual tension exhaling from your body. Breathe in again, collecting out last residual tension, and breathe out. One more time, take a deep breath in and the last of your tension is slowly exhaled away and you feel totally relaxed and at ease. Now, I want you to focus on your inner thoughts and start to see your surroundings slowly getting blurrier and fading away.

See yourself walking down a white hallway that has no sounds or colors and as you continue to walk down this hallway you come upon a white door. On this white door is a red doorknob and you see yourself reaching your hand out slowly turning the red doorknob and pushing the door wide open.

As you walk through the doorway, step right into the environment that you created for yourself and the full expression of your core value. You can see yourself doing things that are necessary to really enhance this value. The environment around you is vibrant and you can see the colors around you in great detail. You notice how you feel from an emotional state as you are fully expressing the core value that you have right now. The sounds around you slowly begin to intensify as you slowly turn the dial up and add more sound to the environment. You can hear your own voice as you are talking about your core value to yourself, experiencing the emotion and the senses that come up as you continue to express it.

Listen closely. Let me ask you, how are you feeling right now? What emotions are you experiencing? You stand still for a moment and fully envelop all the feelings and emotions that you're experiencing right now, and you let them overwhelm you. Pay attention to all your senses currently. Look around and not only do you see yourself, but you see others around you, augmenting the core value within you. You hear yourself talking to them with back and forth communication as well as seeing others talk to themselves in conversation. Listen to the conversations that you are hearing right now from yourself and from others around you.

You continue to hear yourself talking and hear the voices around you, feeling your emotions and fully expressing them at this time. You're seeing your environment in great detail, seeing the vivid colors and shapes of the people and the environment within. And now, around you, start to see that time begins to slow down and the sounds and conversations begin to diminish in intensity. Time is moving so slowly that everything in your environment appears to stand still and there is a quiet and peace because the only sound that you can hear is your inner voice.

You begin to feel yourself as light as a feather and are totally relaxed without any tension and you begin to feel your body slowly drifting away as time continues to stand still. Even though you are floating away you see your body still standing in the same location, frozen in time with the rest of your environment. Imagine yourself hovering above, seeing your body and your environment with even more clarity.

As you are drifting above, right in front of you, you see a silver doorknob floating in front of you. You slowly reach out and gently turn that knob. As you begin to turn it, the sounds around you which are now silent begin to intensify and you can hear yourself and all the people around you with much more clarity. As the sound intensifies, the environment, yourself, and the people around you begin to move again. You're above yourself, observing how you express your core value and your interactions with your environment. You are paying very close attention to what you are saying and doing, continuing to act within the vivid environment around you. And as you are floating above yourself, watching and observing everything in detail, you begin to feel a little bit heavier and you slowly drift back down towards your body. And as you connect again with your body you begin to feel the emotions and the feelings that are expressed as you continue to express your core value.

You slowly turn around and you see the door behind you where you first entered. You gradually walk back towards it, remembering all your senses and emotions and feelings that you just experienced. As you reach out to turn the doorknob, it slowly opens, and you begin to walk through. You hear the door slowly close behind you and then hear a final click as it closes. You are back in the white hallway feeling calm and relaxed.

How was this exercise for you when expressing your core value?

Were you able to incorporate your senses, feelings, and emotions as you had a full expression of the core value that you desired within yourself?

One of the most powerful ways to make this more effective would be to create your own script that is much more specific in taking you through all the senses, emotions, and feelings regarding the core value and then recording it in your own voice. When you do that, listening to your voice guide you through your scenario, it's going to be much more powerful and effective for you in time.

Now this visualization was shorter than the first two because I can only provide you with so much detail because everybody that reads this is obviously going to have a different core value that they wish to express.

Feel free to make this script for yourself as short or long as you desire. The length of the script is irrelevant. The only thing that matters is that it is effective for you and allows you to maximize your senses, emotions, and feelings.

Take the time right now to start writing your visualization script for your core value. Since you just completed the exercise, the visualization is still fresh in your mind and I encourage you to start creating your script at this time while the imagery is still vivid. If you feel reading your script to yourself allows you to experience your senses, emotions, and feelings then by all means you may read the script. However, in my experience, and the experience of those that I have taught these visualization techniques to, it is much more powerful when you have your eyes closed and you are hearing your own voice guide you through the visualization.

Before you move to the next building block exercise, take the time to have this complete and then I would encourage you to practice it multiple times and really lock it in, as you did for the first two visualization techniques.

Building Block 4: Seeing Yourself Achieve Your Outcome

In this visualization building block, you're going to experience visualizing your outcomes and I'm going to create a visualization for you that is so powerful that it will seem as if it's your current reality. The overall outcome that you will achieve for these visualizations is to have a picture in your mind of your future goals and outcomes that looks, sounds, and feels as if it exists in the present time. Remember, your subconscious does not understand or care about the difference between reality and fantasy so it is to your advantage to be as creative and vivid as possible, implanting that visualization within your subconscious, which in turn allows you to act consciously and subconsciously in ways that will move you forward towards your desired outcome.

I can't design a visualization script for you specifically since everyone who reads this book will have their own outcomes that they desire. That's why you can and should develop your own visualization scripts. It is fun, exciting, and more powerful to design your personalized visualization script and work through it like the models that I provided above. The key is keeping your mind open, being as creative and vivid as possible with regards to your visualization.

You already have the initial portion of the visualization script to start with, which is the portion where you are sitting calm and relaxed and I'm taking you through exercises that involve deep breathing, relaxation, and alleviation of tension. However, if there is a situation or wording that better serves you, putting you in an even more calm and relaxed state, I encourage you to do so.

After that portion, you can choose to be in a void and empty white hallway which opens into your newly visualized world or you can skip this transition altogether and once you are in a calm and relaxed state, instantly begin to visualize the outcome that you desire.

Here's a **sample visualization** with the simulated outcome of a man who has lost 20 pounds in 90 days. Let's assume that you are already in a relaxed state and I am going directly into the visualization itself. It could look something like this:

Visualization scenario 4

You are looking at yourself in the mirror and are amazed at the transformation that you have had in the last 90 days. Looking at your physical reflection, it warms your heart and brings a smile to your face as you look and feel 20 years younger. You feel so excited to have gotten to the point that you desired 90 days ago, despite the challenges and the setbacks. You pushed through your regimen of diet and exercise, remained disciplined with your plan, and now get to experience the fruits of your labor. As you leave the restroom at the beach and start to walk upon the cool sand you realize how much energy you have and how physically fit you feel.

Not feeling short of breath and winded just brings a smile to your face and warms your heart. And as you walk towards your family members, they may look back at you with smiles and admiration, particularly your wife, having a beautiful glow about her and smiling ear to ear as she gazes with loving eyes upon you. As you run after the kids and take a swim in the ocean you begin to realize that you're able to keep up with them stroke for stroke without being winded. You feel alive and energetic as the cool blue water makes effortless ripples as you swim each stroke with ease.

This is the moment that was all worth it!

And as your kids go back to shore and run back to your wife, you take a seat on the big beach towel blanket as your wife opens the mahogany colored weaved basket and begins to take out healthy snacks for everybody to enjoy. Foods that you thought a mere 90 days ago you would never eat are just so tasty and healthy. Reflecting upon how you used to think of eating things like this brings you into an uncontrollable laugh that has everybody turning their heads on the beach and looking at you. Standing up with confidence and giving a little muscle flex for the people that are looking back at you, you have a sense of accomplishment and an overwhelming feeling of confidence knowing that all your hard work paid off. Then time begins to slow down for you just for a fraction of a second, allowing you to float out of your body and see the clear and expansive beach from the sky above.

You see the three other couples and their families that you invited to the beach with you on this weekend. You see the fellas looking at you, amazed on how fit and healthy you look. As you guys talk back and forth you see that the guys are really interested in the tips and techniques that you share with them. You start to feel their excitement about wanting to get fit just like you.

And as you start to flow back down into your body, feeling the warmth of the sun on your skin, looking around at all your family and friends as they smile back, you feel overwhelmed with joy that you not only made a difference in your life but in the lives of those who are closest to you.

Visualization script number four should be able to provide you with the template to help guide you towards creating your own visualization script for your outcomes. Now, I want you to pull out your sheet of your three written outcomes that you placed to the side and choose one of the outcomes that you wish to practice your visualization with. This time you are going to write a visualization script and then focus on visualizing the outcome. You are going to see yourself at the endpoint completing the outcome at hand, focusing on maximizing your senses, feelings, and emotions.

Here are some key questions and tips that will help you create a complete visualization for your one outcome:

Where are you at and what do you see, feel, and hear around you?

How do you physically see yourself?

What is the emotion that you have with completing your outcome?

If you need some guidance, reflect upon your core values that you established in the first trimester and incorporate the emotions that can represent these core values.

How does it feel to visualize yourself overcoming the challenges and obstacles that are holding you back from your desired outcomes?

What family, friends, or people, in general, are around your situation or outcome, and how are they interacting with you?

Enhance the details of the scene around you, such as the colors and shapes of objects and their sizes. Feel free to play around with them to augment the visualization. Imagine seeing yourself in the third person. Either by floating above you, as you did in the above examples. Or, you can be creative like looking at your life as if it were playing in a movie theater and you are the only person in the audience.

Are you moving through your environment? Are you standing still, running, or walking? Are you talking with yourself or with others around you and how are you interacting with the environment around you?

As you finished reading the visualization tips and questions, having gone through the previous visualization scripts, and continuing to absorb the words of the chapter, you will come to realize that visualization is not as hard as you thought in the past and it will be quite an enjoyable event for you.

Practice, practice, practice!!!

When you first do this, like all new things in life, there will be a learning curve and challenges. But in time, and with a lot of practice and repetition, you will get there! I encourage you to practice visualization a minimum of twice a day. I use visualization not only for my goals and outcomes but for anything that I wish to see myself being successful in. The possibilities for using the technique are endless.

Let's look at the outcome in a different way. Instead of seeing it as an end point, look at it as a waypoint, a pitstop on a never-ending path. When you look at it this way, you will realize that the journey along your path is filled with not just one outcome, but multiple outcomes.

It's like your main outcome (like one of the three that you created) has sub-outcomes (goals).

Take, for example, having an outcome of losing 20 pounds in 90 days. This represents your main outcome, the one that you will visualize about each day. However, you can add sub-outcomes within this as well. For example, the sub-outcome could be seeing yourself successfully complete all your workouts for the week or completing your meal plan for the day. Now, you may be thinking "man, that's a ton of outcomes and visualizations to do each day."

Well, how bad do you want your outcomes in the first place?

Yes, it will take time at first but as you practice more, you are going to become quicker and more efficient with the visualizations because they will become more focused and detailed. It's not about the time, it's about the realism of the visualization with its associated senses, feelings, and emotions. In time, it may literally take you only 60 seconds to have the powerful visualization that serves you at that moment in time!

Practicing for your upcoming REBIRTH

The exciting part is now upon you! Preparing for your rebirth and delivering the enhanced version of yourself. It is this newly delivered you that will be prepared to take the next step in your Circle of Conception.

Taking Action!

Now, the time is upon you to really drill down on the three categories of outcomes, determining which ones will best serve you to start, and formulating the plans that will move you along your path towards achieving them. As you do this, you will learn skills to make your time more efficient, create rituals that will fuel you throughout the day, and applications that will streamline your effectiveness in achieving your outcomes.

Take the time to reflect upon all that you have learned until this point.

Your **preconception care** helped you bust your **limiting beliefs** and develop your powerful **WHY**, providing you with the powerful answers that will keep you determined along your path towards your outcome.

Your **first trimester** was the first step within the **Circle of Conception** and provided the building blocks of the person of who you wish to **BE**. Enhancing your focus, developing your core values, opening your mind for the possibilities of thinking along multiple time lines and states of being.

As you flowed through the **second trimester**, you transitioned from the person that you wished to BE towards what you needed to internally **DO** in order to overcome your fears and obstacles. Conquering the roadblocks as you flowed through **The F.E.A.R. Cycle**, slowly chipping away at it, gaining the confidence and determination that is essential for flowing towards your outcomes.

The **third trimester** helped you **SEE** the future version of yourself, having achieved your outcomes. You developed powerful visualizations that will train your subconscious as if you have already achieved your outcomes today!

Congratulate yourself for being patient with the process because you have a quality within you that many people do not. When going through this flow with others, I have had a few tell me, "Terence, just teach me the system of getting the goals and outcomes and forget the rest, I don't need it."

It reminds me of some patients that want to be induced as soon as they hit 35 or 36 weeks of pregnancy. Telling me, "I'm done and I'm ready to stop being pregnant." I can understand the discomfort they go through and see how uncomfortable or in pain they might be, but all things happen for a reason. Even at this time, delivering the babies may have unforeseen consequences of prematurity like difficulty breathing after their deliveries. Unless there is a major medical issue, I tell my patients that it is better to go into labor naturally rather than for me force the process with medications.

The same applies with your progress towards your outcomes.

Yes, I could have skipped the BE, DO and SEE, just giving you the next section and call it a day. But the physician in me is here to provide you with the optimal care during your own mental growth and the last thing I want before your own rebirth is to have you deliver a version of yourself which is premature and undeveloped.

And yes, the process has taken time but in the long run, you are much better equipped to move forward with your reborn self, allowing you to flow even faster and more efficiently towards your desired outcomes.

So, with that being said, congratulations on completing your third trimester within the Circle of Conception.

Welcome to the next phase of your development:

Your REBIRTH!

Chapter 11
Your Delivery: REBIRTH and Learning How to "Act"

Congratulations to you!

I don't know if you realize how much progress you have made until this time! Finally, you have entered the stage of your rebirth.

This is the time where you utilize all your development during your level one foundation and the various components within level two, your focus and Circle of Conception. Your circle is now arriving at its conclusion and it time to continue to move forward and get what you desire.

It's time to act!

In the traditional model of Be, Do, and Have, people may describe "Do" as the action step that gets you forward however, I have found that this definition tends to be flawed and incomplete because its action wasn't defined enough for me. DO is the **internal action** for overcoming fear and ACT is the **external action** that drives you towards your outcomes.

Let's face it, many of us know what we need to do in order to achieve the results that we desire.

For example, we know that we need to focus on diet and exercise for weight loss.

The problem is not the lack of understanding or information. The internet is flooded with thousands of ways to approach your diet for weight loss. The amount of exercise and workout routines that you can research and do is overwhelming. You can't make the excuse that you don't know what to do because if you dig deep enough, you will find it.

Most likely you know how to lose weight, in this example. You probably have a sense on how to start the process that will get you the goals and outcomes that you desire in your life. But pay attention because here is the powerful question for you:

Do you know how to act or take action?

Therefore, this module is critical as you enter your rebirth. My mission is to guide you with your newly developed tools and techniques that you developed within your preconception care and circle of life and help you take action by using them as support, moving you forward towards the goals and outcomes that you desire.

There are many things that I will do during your rebirth phase to help nurture you in your journey.

I will define action and you will understand its importance for your growth moving forward. Once this is understood, getting you in the correct mindset for taking action, the next step will be systemizing a plan that is specific to you, allowing you to complete your flow towards the outcomes that you desire personally, socially and financially.

It used to be thought that a habit can be locked in in just 21 days, however, current research suggests otherwise. On average, it takes a person 66 days, triple the originally thought time, to lock in a pattern that will form a habit.

The original concept for the 21 days is based on the observations of a plastic surgeon in the 1950s named Maxwell Maltz. He noticed with himself and his patients that habits would form within a minimal time of 21 days. However, over the years, his definition has been skewed by the gurus, who twisted the definition from a minimum of 21 days to only 21 days.

A subtle difference, yet very powerful, because the implication was that changes in habits only required 21 days to change. Dr. Maltz's research showed it took a MINIMUM of 21 days, not EXACTLY 21 days.

So, the real answer of the time behind habit formation was enhanced with a study from London, published in the European Journal of Social Psychology, authored by Phillippa Lally. It shows that it takes, on average, 66 days to make a habit stick, triple the originally thought time.

If you desire, I will provide you with a simplified template for you taking action towards your goals and outcomes for a 90-day window. Once you have completed the actions that move you towards your outcomes in 90 days, you will begin to realize the power of creating a solid habit, allowing you to take on any new goals, outcomes and desires more efficiently and effectively.

I'm excited for you right now!

Your level of commitment towards developing the enhanced version of you is amazing because you are doing what the majority of people won't do.

Having patience and trusting the process.

Congratulate yourself now and give yourself a pat on the shoulder. Yes, it may seem silly to you but as I stated before, you don't wait until you achieve your goals and outcomes. As you take each step forward, as you complete each action necessary, be excited for your progress and understand this:

You are in a space, a mindset, that 90% of people can't or won't have the courage to take on.

Defining action

Many others that teach taking action will state the obvious, telling you to just take a step forward and do the damn thing, however, it's a disservice to you for me to do that. Don't get me wrong, it is important to do this but there is another component that you need to comprehend first. So, let's not look at taking action but approaching it from the standpoint of why you DON'T act. Once you understand why you DON'T take action, it will facilitate you more towards taking it going forward.

For many years, well decades I should say, I have practiced medicine, delivering the precious little ones, and providing quality obstetric and gynecologic care for thousands of patients. It's been an amazing 22-year journey (as of the time of writing this book), and it's a path that I would choose again if I had the opportunity to turn back time and start over. However, after 15 years of being in the field, coupled with my abrupt termination with a previous employer because I didn't make their financial cut, I began to realize that there was a second important component that allowed me to stay so long in the field.

The income that I have been able to generate was wonderful for myself and supporting my family. It allowed me to take the vacations that I desired, travel to see family, and have the stuff in life that I thought would sustain my happiness. All of this, combined with the love for the job and patients, drove me but there was something deeper that I wanted but never pursued.

What was that component that held me back from pursuing my passions, you ask?

I was comfortable.

And likely, so are you.

So why was I comfortable? It's because our brains, through thousands of years of evolution, were designed to keep us safe. Thousands of years ago, that safety mechanism was important because it allowed us to avoid danger with predators that could kill us, other tribes that wanted our resources, and take actions that were in our best interests for survival.

Today, we don't have to worry about a tiger leaping out of the alley to eat us (but a man with a weapon leaping at us in the middle of the night is still a hazard). Our brains have retained the defensive mechanism to keep us safe, the fight or flight mechanism that we discussed earlier in the book.

Fight or flight is buried neurologically within the amygdala of our brain and keeps us safe as it is triggered when there is any perceived danger to ourselves, causing a chain reaction within our physical, mental, and emotional selves.

For me, my brain kept me safe as I enjoyed the lifestyle of the job that I had. And when I had thoughts of wanting to do something different, my fight or flight would kick in. Not to keep me from dying, like in ancient times, but to keep me comfortable.

I was comfortable with having a "steady" income.

I was comfortable with having the "status" of being a physician.

I was comfortable with knowing that I was helping my community and patients, serving others for the greater good.

Thus, when I thought outside the box, having the thoughts of wanting to make a change in my life, the fight or flight kicked in, triggering waves of discomfort with fear, self-doubt, confusion, and indecision.

It wasn't my fault because my ancient neurologic patterns were keeping me safe and they are keeping you safe as well.

So, you ask, "How do I take action and move forward if my mind is keeping me safe?"

The key is to learn how to break out of your comfortable loop that you are living in.

No, it's not as easy as it sounds, and it will take work, but once you do it, not only will you take the action that is necessary to achieve your goals and outcomes, you will begin the process that will vastly improve your life!

Understanding your comfort loop

Understand this point and pay close attention:

We are always in a continuous loop, the exception being the times that we break away from our existing loop in order to make a subtle shift towards a new one.

Do you remember my initial story in the beginning of the book where I talked about having the fear of drowning? Remember the panic attacks that I experienced during my first open water swims? I was in a loop of not progressing my swimming skills because the fight or flight response was trying to keep me safe, reminding me of the fear of drowning and not giving me the chance to progress forward.

Really ugly!

Today, I swim in the open water and don't give it a second thought, yet I am still in a loop.

Let me explain.

The fear of drowning was a loop because for years, decades actually, the fears kept me from *even wanting to learn* how to swim. Then, I shifted into a new loop, the desire to get better, once I reflected on my past failures and sat determined in my car to swim (or drown trying) before my breakout race. Finally, I am in the current loop where I am comfortable with open water swimming and have minimal fear of it now.

Life is about loops. We are constantly within them, except when we **break them or expand upon** the current one that we are in.

I think of the transition out of the first loop as **breaking** it because, for me, it was a big shift from not wanting to swim to attempting open water races. Thus, I broke the first loop and entered the second one.

The transformation within the second loop was more about **expansion**. I overcame the fear of refusing to learn to swim towards being in the water, *breaking the first loop*. The transition from panic attacks in the open water towards swimming comfortably was an *expansion of the second loop*.

I bring this up because for some things in your life, for some of your goals and desired outcomes, you will either:

Break your existing loop and make that subtle shift to a new one, or

Expand upon your existing loop, growing it to a new level of comfort.

Remember this, with either breaking or expanding, you are still moving out of your comfortable loop pattern, creating a new one that will become a habit that's solidified with time. It becomes your new comfortable loop.

The challenging part is altering your loop by taking physical action and that's what this section will help do, by guiding you through it!

There is absolutely nothing wrong with being comfortable. The problem occurs when it's been months, years, and decades from the last time that you broke or expanded upon the previous loop that got you to where you are today.

Life is about constantly growing and expanding yourself. Shifting your loops of being comfortable in order to grow into the enhanced version of yourself. You don't have to take *massive* action, unless you choose to. Only a small shift is required to build the momentum, moving you forward with the action necessary to do what needs to be done!

Think about the game of baseball. Despite growing up in New York, I've only been to one Yankees game in my life (but that's another story)! Have you ever heard of or seen the team manager getting pissed off because someone got on base with a single?

Probably not!

However, hitting a single doesn't count as a score?

Or does it?

Now, for the hard-core fans who want to say, "Well if the bases are loaded, a run comes in," just relax and work with me.

Hitting singles builds the momentum for the team, inspiring other players to duplicate the process and get as many people on the bases. Because when the doubles, triples, and home runs are hit with someone already on base, the runs start adding up.

You are looking to hit singles and not swing for the fences. Building up your momentum by taking small action steps, loading up your confidence, because when you hit the homerun, you now get a greater reward.

Again, **massive action** helps but it's not essential.

I will take singles all day long because I know with enough of them, my runs will come in, achieving my desired goals and outcomes.

You may have not realized it, but since you are at this stage in the book, I have provided you with three powerful singles that will help you either break your current loop or expand upon it by taking action.

These singles are the building blocks for creating the momentum necessary to take the action that is required.

Because you have already learned how to hit singles, you are able to start building the momentum, which leads to taking action, which leads to more self-confidence, which leads to a higher level of accomplishment, pushing you even closer towards your desired goals and outcomes.

So, what are these singles and what skills do we use to trigger them?

Asking the Right Questions

Moving to act is about asking yourself the right questions. You will soon learn what those powerful questions are and how they are linked to the three singles that you have already learned. You may ask, when did I learn them and what are they? You will discover that shortly! Basically, you are going to load the bases for yourself. Imagine this, hitting three singles in your game of life so that the action that you take scores a run for you.

Exciting stuff!

Like I said previously, it would be a disservice to you to just tell you to act. Yes, that will work in some cases, but we are looking for action to work most of the time for you. Thus, when the action is pre-framed with the right question, it becomes so much more powerful. You are a major league superstar, taking action at the plate, having that initial confidence to step up to it. But what earns you the right to even get on the field is practice.

Lots and lots of it!

Your practice for your upcoming action has come in the form of taking the time to do the exercises throughout the book. Everything has a purpose within this book and your practice during your preconception, circle of life, and current stage of rebirth, has prepared you for the next step that you are about to take now.

The first and one of the most powerful questions that you ask yourself is this:

Do I wish to live in the same loop or do I wish to break or expand upon it?

It's not taking the action to break the loop but getting you to see your life where it is, understand that you're in a loop of being comfortable, and making the micro commitment to move towards breaking it.

Again, breaking or stretching your existing loop is a key component for taking action. Some people will take massive action and do a serious break of the loop while many of us will simply stretch it. If you are the one who stretches it, that's wonderful!

Every action that moves you forward towards an enhanced version of you is great because you have initiated the process to get closer towards your goals and outcomes.

Understand this, being in the loop is not the problem. The problem is not making the commitment to transition to a new loop or expand upon the current one. A loop that is higher and more rewarding than your existing one. Because when you have moved forward by taking action and are comfortable in your new loop, you will realize, like I did with swimming, that the new loop feels comfortable and natural for you.

How does knowing your why and having a vision help you?

This trio of questions is a self-check to make sure you are still on your path towards the outcomes that you desire. Think of the questions as a miniaturized version of your development from the beginning. *What's my seven level deep why?* The question reflects upon your preconception care and brings you back to the basics of your development. *What core values do I wish to express?* It was your development through level two of the Circle of Conception, your first trimester growth. Finally, *what do I visualize my future as?* Utilize the powerful visualization techniques developed in you third trimester.

Thus, think of the three questions as a cheat sheet to remind you of the growth that you have had and the waypoints that will keep you going.

These are the three singles that will get you in the game and eventually score!

The second way these questions help you is when you get stuck, particularly in taking action. Like the person who knows how to diet and exercise for weight loss but doesn't take the action to do so, these questions will serve you as a trigger to hit the singles, get on base, and move forward in your own game of life towards your goals and outcomes.

So, when I don't feel like waking up at 4:45 in the morning to practice swimming, when I am looking at that piece of dessert or food that I shouldn't have, the questions help me take the necessary action that I need. I remember **"why"** I decided to train for triathlons and stay fit, leading by example and staying congruent with my teachings. My **core values** of determination and confidence remind me of the strong leader that I am, knowing that others are looking at me as a model for their own success. My **visualization** keeps me forward thinking, seeing the long-term outcome in my mind as being complete, and allowing me not to settle for the short-term benefits or quick rewards.

Inaction is one of the biggest roadblocks that holds people back from delivering an enhanced version of themselves, but not you! You have learned about the three questions, reading them to yourself and knowing where they came from in your developmental cycle. Now, your chances of taking action are significantly enhanced over the average person who says to themselves, or listens to others who say, "Go for it, take big action and just keep going."

That's all great but that ra-ra-ra is only a temporary high that keeps you going for a few days or weeks. A few months if you are lucky. Therefore, you see some people fall off after going to personal development conferences, because many times, it hypes you up but is a short-term fix.

I'm not into short-term fixes for you. I'm into giving you the tools for long-term growth and development. Thus, when you feel stuck, unmotivated, confused, or fearful, reflect upon the three questions that will have you hit the singles, taking small action steps forward and staying in the game for a much longer period of time.

Changing your comfort loop

Now with the powerful questions in your arsenal, let's revisit your *comfort loop*.

Previously, we discussed that we are all within a loop, which determines our daily habits, patterns, and actions (or the opposite, inaction). The challenge that you face is getting out of the loop by acting and the trio of powerful questions will help you take the action that's necessary to get closer towards your desired outcomes and goals.

Understand that there is power in changing your comfort loop, more specifically, upgrading it. This is done through either expansion of the existing loop *or* breaking the loop and creating a new one. The questions will help you take the necessary action but let's explore your loop even more closely because when you do, you will begin to see a pattern in your life, giving you even more insight and determination to alter your comfort loop.

You were not born with the comfort loop that you are in. At some point in your life, you had an experience which changed the way that you think and live. It could have been getting a better job, causing you to put your real dreams on hold because now things are financially stable. There may have been a relationship that was mentally, emotionally, or physically traumatic for you that caused you not to socially engage as you had done in the past.

These experiences are what I define as a L.E.A.P.

Learning to L.E.A.P. forward!

Defined as Life Evolving Affective Pinnacles, L.E.A.P.(s) are the emotional events that are so powerful, in time they trigger your subconscious to accept the new situation as reality. So, the excitement of the job may trigger complacency or safety, never striving to grow yourself more. The sadness or frustration of the failed relationship may trigger being more reclusive, untrusting of others, and being more introverted. Good or bad, our L.E.A.P.(s) in life set our comfort loops. When you recognize the L.E.A.P. you will understand the comfort loop that you are in and how you are driving it. Because once you understand your loop, you can make the decision internally to alter it, moving forward with the trio of questions that will allow you to take action externally.

Now, you are beginning to understand your loop and you have the powerful questions needed to stimulate you to act. The biggest question remains, "What is the level of action that you wish to make?" Before, we discussed looking at your loop in two ways, either by expanding the comfort loop or breaking the comfort loop and creating a new and higher level of comfort. When I look at these two types of altered loops, I simplify the process by reflecting on the level of action that I want to make.

If it's an action that I wish to make a major shift (over time of course!) with my outcomes, then I see that as **breaking a loop** because it potentially causes a major shift in my life. For example, transitioning from the comfort loop of an Obstetrician of 22 years with the steady job to a full-time entrepreneur would represent a break of my loop. Obviously, my lifestyle—mentally, physically, emotionally, and spiritually—would involve some major shifts.

If it's an action that I wish to make smaller shifts with my outcomes, then I see that as **expanding a loop** because the comfort pattern may be similar, yet it is altered in a way that enhances my life. For example, being healthy and working out five days per week, then adding weight training two times a week would represent an expansion of my comfort loop. I'm still in a similar comfort pattern of exercise, just expanding upon it.

Some people can take on major shifts in their life and their actions would represent the breaking of their loops. Others may take smaller actions, maybe not as big but still profound enough for them, with a shift in their comfort loop, representing an expansion of it. The level of action that you wish to take is totally dependent upon you! No matter how small it is, if it moves you forward—understand that is an action that will vastly improve your life!

The takeaway is that action is the step that grows you. After going through your preconception care and the circle of life, you have developed yourself into a powerful being. And now with your rebirth, this "act" stage is the key to your continued growth. Because I have seen many people give up on their dreams because of a lack of action, I want to stress its importance to you because you are worth it!

The myths of taking action

Before we get into the next stage of selecting your outcomes and learning how to execute them, let's talk about some of the misconceptions of taking action, shall we!

"You must have confidence before you take action."

We previously addressed this when talking about overcoming fear. Much of your confidence builds after you start taking action, not before it. I have read and heard others say that you must have a massive amount of confidence before taking that first step and that is simply not true. I remember the first time I went into the lake and had my first swim lesson there. Now, I had on a full wetsuit, providing me with the buoyancy to stay afloat. Consciously, I knew this, but subconsciously, the panic alarms went off, overwhelming me with fear. Was I confident that day in the lake? Hell no! But the most important thing was taking action. Even though I only swam 100 yards before returning to shore, I still swam 100 yards. Is that as much as when I would swim 2000 yards plus in the pool? Not at all. The size of the action didn't matter. What mattered is taking the action. It was small yet powerful because I built the confidence each time I got back into the lake to practice. Remember, you may be scared out of your wits taking action but understand that your actions, no matter how small, compound upon one another, allowing you to build your confidence over time.

"You have to fake it until you make it"

I am all about having congruency between the internal person that you believe you are and the external person that you wish to be seen as. I have never liked the negative connotation of "fake it until you make it" because there are people who "fake" it and that is a good thing.

Let me explain.

During my years as a physician, speaking to others was natural to me because I would speak to hundreds of patients, month after month in the office and in the hospital. However, as I began my transition to entrepreneurship, I migrated to speaking to larger and larger groups. It was challenging for me at first, being looked at by many more people, but as time went on, I became more comfortable with it. Did I "fake" being confident with public speaking? Yes, because I needed to present a position of authority and confidence. It's challenging to change people's lives if they see and feel that you're not confident in yourself. So yes, initially my public speaking may not have had 100% genuine confidence at the time. The more important thing is that I took the action to overcome the challenge and move closer towards my desired outcome. The point is, don't think of "faking it" as a negative thing, especially if you are taking action to alter your comfort loop.

"Opportunity only comes once"

Some feel that when opportunity knocks on their door, they must drop everything and act right then. Again, a misconception put forth by people who lack vision. Opportunity is around you and knocks, sometimes bangs, on your door multiple times. The question is this: are you paying attention to the knocking? Those who say opportunity only knocks once only can see an outcome for their lives in one way and hastily jump in when they see it. It's great they act but if you don't have a plan and an outcome, it's a recipe for disaster. Keeping your mind open to the possibilities, having that positive attitude regarding your actions and outcomes, you will begin to realize that opportunity is all around you and you just need to decide how that action affects your current comfort loop and how it can potentially change it for the better.

So, don't fret when you miss an opportunity. Opportunities will come, so just look for the signs of them. Remember, action doesn't have to be massive and instantaneous because even the smaller opportunities and actions will serve you just as well.

Let's act upon your outcomes!

During the second trimester of your growth, you initiated the process of creating nine outcomes that you desired at the time. Now, after completing your full development and growth, having been reborn and learning how to take action, it's time to fine tune your outcomes now!

During the second trimester, you developed and wrote your outcomes.

If you need a refresher, feel free to review the section on developing outcomes in Chapter 7 or simply download the worksheets for "Develop Your Outcomes" at:

https://www.docdeliversbooks.com/free-ebook/

With your outcomes in hand, I want you to reflect upon them and select the ONE outcome from each category that you feel you would like to conquer first. After having your final three, the next step is making them specific and for that, we will utilize a time-tested method for this, the "S.M.A.R.T." Technique.

Understanding the S.M.A.R.T. Technique

Another way to think about your outcomes is by writing them down in a S.M.A.R.T. format. This is how I've been able to maintain my motivation and accomplish so much more than before. So, what makes a S.M.A.R.T. outcome smart?

It is Specific, Measurable, Achievable, Relevant, and Time-bound. Here is its mnemonic:

S – Specific
M – Measurable
A – Achievable
R – Relevant
T – Time-bound

Outcomes that are Specific, Measurable, Achievable, Relevant, and Time-bound are a systemized way of structuring your goals, providing you with a system that gives you a roadmap to success. It's the gift that keeps on giving.

Now, many people think or believe that you can just have a plan in your head and execute it effectively. But that's not very likely. Writing your plan down makes it real. It makes it a tangible thing. It acts as a step-by-step guide to achievement. With the correct plan, you can successfully achieve in 90 days what takes most people an entire year. Or even longer.

How is this possible? That's what I'm about to show you. Let's talk about steps of planning out your S.M.A.R.T. outcomes, which will provide the template for setting up your 90-day path towards the enhanced version of you! First, you have to breakdown the plan using the S.M.A.R.T. Technique. So, let's dig a little deeper into each of the requirements.

S is for... Specific

For an outcome to be "specific," it must be well defined and clear to anyone that reads it. But more importantly, it must be clear to you. Because you are the one who chooses to do it! Notice, I didn't say *have* to, I said *choose* to. The goal is not something to check off a bucket list. It should be something you embrace. It should also serve a purpose to you. Why do you want to achieve your outcome and how will it benefit you and those around you?

M is for... Measurable

For an outcome to be measurable, it must be well defined with a specific endpoint. There must be a "finish line" so you are 100% sure when it is complete. By measurable, I mean that the outcome can be observed, assessed, and calculated. In short, make your outcomes quantifiable. An outcome of "losing 10 lbs. in 90 days" is far less ambiguous than "getting in shape." Measurable outcomes assist not only with achievement, but accountability as well.

A is for... Achievable

Make sure your outcome is achievable, meaning it is within the realm of possibility. Base it on your current situation and where you are at currently. It should stretch you but still be obtainable. Realistic outcomes are accomplishable ones. Setting impossible outcomes won't serve you in the long run. It's self-defeating and leads to a lot of negativity. Wanting to "lose 10 lbs. in 90 days" is one thing. Wanting to "grow three inches in 90 days" is definitely not achievable.

But be careful you don't throw out a bold outcome just because others think it can't be done. The outcomes are about you, first and foremost.

R is for... Relevant

Does the outcome align with your established core values? Will achieving it move you closer to your long-term visualization of the future version of yourself? Don't waste your time on an outcome that isn't helping you progress.

An outcome to "lose 10 lbs. in 90 days" doesn't make much sense to a chef experimenting with new recipes on the brink of opening his or her first restaurant. Non-relevant outcomes have the potential to set you up for failure. Not because you can't attain them. It's more along the lines of "who cares if we do?" The answer is "you care." If the outcome doesn't align with your long-term vision that you have of yourself, it's probably not one that serves you best.

T is for... Timely

Can your outcome be tracked and completed by a specific date? Set hard dates to hit your outcomes and then take the physical step to mark them on the calendar. As you learn the upcoming 90-day plan for your outcomes, you will take the next step in your plans and proceed with breaking up your outcomes into smaller milestones or checkpoints. There will be weekly and monthly ones that you will create. These mini targets and wins will keep you on the path to achievement.

So there you have it. The S.M.A.R.T. outcome system!

When used properly, S.M.A.R.T. outcomes give you a solid plan of actionable steps to follow through. Think of all the goals you've had in your lifetime. Are you the person you dreamed of being more? What prevented you from following through on any of your goals?

What would you do if you had the tools to accomplish any outcome, not in a few years, but in as little as a few months? Let's look at how I might accomplish that with an example of having an outcome of being more physically fit and losing 20 pounds in 90 days.

So, the outcome would be worded as: "My outcome is to lose 20 pounds in 90 days."

Next, as we run it through the S.M.A.R.T. checklist, we have the following:

Specific – the outcome is clearly stated with a specific number in pounds and not as simply "lose weight."

Measurable – This can be clearly measured because there is a target of 20 pounds

Achievable – It's realistic to say you can lose this amount in 90 days. A goal of losing 100 pounds, however, would not.

Relevant – The relevance would depend on a few factors. Is the outcome in line with your core values? For example, if your core values included fitness or health, this would be a relevant outcome.

Timely – This criterion is met because there is a well-defined time frame for completion.

There you have it. A S.M.A.R.T. outcome will allow you to take action that is efficient, moving you closer towards the enhanced version of you. It sets you up for success and keeps you motivated along the way. And most importantly, because it's trackable, you will see the results and milestones as you move forward.

Having reviewed the template for the S.M.A.R.T. outcome, now is the time to pull out your three final outcomes, personal, social, and financial and apply the S.M.A.R.T. checklist to each one of them. Take your time, don't rush the process and overwhelm yourself right out of the gate. Success doesn't happen overnight, but progress happens anytime you're moving towards your well-defined outcome. I remember the first time I worked on S.M.A.R.T. outcomes many years ago and it took me a full three weeks to get them right. However, I didn't have the tools and techniques like you have now. Trust me when I say this, so pay attention! If you don't put your focus and energy into this process, you may realize 45 days in that one of the components of the S.M.A.R.T. outcome is off, causing you lost time and even worse, getting frustrated with the process.

I've been there!

So, let's focus on you getting it correct the first time out.

For a worksheet on creating your three S.M.A.R.T. goals, you can go to:

https://www.docdeliversbooks.com/free-ebook/

and scroll down to the section called "Creating your S.M.A.R.T. Outcomes."

Overview of Your 90-Day Outcome Plan System

When I designed my 90-day plan, I had several desired outcomes. First, I wanted to make it simple and efficient. Instead of having a time sheet that defines every single moment of your day, I have three simplified time blocks that will be the focus for your outcomes. Second, the system focuses more on hitting weekly goals instead of daily ones. I'm not saying that it's not important to have daily targets because they are within the system. My emphasis is upon completing the weekly targets. Let's face it. Sometimes, unexpected events may come up during our day, making it challenging to achieve the outcome we intended. The way my system is designed, by having more emphasis on weekly targets, it takes the pressure off having to hit a goal or outcome every single day.

Now, this comes with the understanding that slacking off is NOT an option. The last thing you should do is have a weekly target date of noon on Sunday, and on Saturday morning you start working on your outcomes for the week at the last minute. Remember Parkinson's law? Yes, I give you a week, but it doesn't mean to wait until the last day! In my personal experience with my own mentor and those that I have mentored myself, I have found that the emphasis upon weekly outcomes allows me to have a much more productive week. It is not uncommon to create my outcomes for the week on Sunday and be completed with them by Tuesday or Wednesday. Now, when this happens, not only am I being efficient, but it allows for me to add bonus outcomes, moving me even faster towards the main outcome that I desire.

Third, I wanted a time course that exceeded 66 days but less than one year. This reflects the previous study by Phillippa Lally. I personally feel, as well as many others, that allowing yourself a year for an outcome opens the door for procrastination and inefficiency. Having the mentality of, "Well, I got 10 months to finish this, so I can put it on hold for a few months," will not serve you. However, having only 90 days allows you to kick the tires and light the fires, igniting the fire under your bottom to take action sooner rather than later.

Why is this important?

Because, during your progress of achieving your outcomes, you will be taking actions that will be repeatable and having the 90-day timeline will provide you with more than enough time for any new habits to stick. Not only for the current outcomes that you desire in the 90-day window but for building habits that could serve you as you progress towards new outcomes beyond.

Overall, the system will run for 90 days with weekly goals that will serve as your checkpoints. But in order to make sure you stay on track with your 90-day outcome, you will also have two monthly expectations that provide broader waypoints for the 90-day outcome. These will be at the conclusion of your first 28 days and then again at the 56-day checkpoint. Again, I don't discount daily targets, I just put more emphasis on the weekly ones, so there will be daily flowsheets that will serve you as well.

Let's simplify the process for our visual people out there:

Daily – Record your "daily actions"

Weekly – Record your "weekly outlooks (or goals)"

Monthly – Record your "monthly expectations"

90-day outcome – Record your "S.M.A.R.T. outcome"

Reverse engineer the 90-day timeline

The most important step is defining your S.M.A.R.T. outcome, which you should have completed at this time. Now that you know what your outcome is, think about breaking it down into three measurable parts. Fortunately, you only have to do two because, if structured correctly, your S.M.A.R.T. outcome itself is already measurable. These are defined as your month one and two "monthly expectations."

Let's take the example of losing 20 pounds in 90 days. For your first and second "monthly expectations," you would have expectations of losing seven pounds by day 28 and losing 14 pounds in total by day 56.

Why is this important? Because your S.M.A.R.T. outcome could be intimidating to you, as you may view it during your journey as being more challenging than you originally realized. It may be overwhelming to think: "I have 20 pounds to lose." However, if you have monthly expectations of seven pounds of weight loss, it makes the task less mentally challenging and more obtainable to you. Also, the monthly expectations will be targets of celebration which we will discuss later in this module. As I have stated during your second trimester, it's critical to celebrate the victories along the way.

To even make the waypoint more manageable for you mentally, your "weekly outlooks" breakdown your "monthly expectations" into more manageable components as well. Thus, you will have weekly outlooks after weeks one, two, three, five, six, seven, nine, 10, and 11. Weeks four and eight represent your monthly expectations and week 12 is your 90-day S.M.A.R.T. outcome finale.

Let's revisit the example of losing 20 pounds in 90 days with a monthly expectation of seven pounds of weight loss at day 28, and second month expectation of losing a total of 14 pounds by day 56. Now, we add the weekly outlooks. For example, you could set weight targets of losing two, four, and six pounds by weeks two, three, and four, respectively. Alternatively, you could set outlook targets related to exercise of working out for one hour, two hours, four hours and then five hours for weeks one, two, three and four, respectively. Also, you could have dietary weekly breakdown involving caloric intake or a combination of all three: weight, exercise, and diet. It's totally up to you!

Typically, after I have determined my S.M.A.R.T. outcome, I first fill in my monthly expectations, followed by my weekly outlooks and I usually do this on a Sunday. I typically stick with planning one month in advance, so I have a clear picture of the targets that need to be done. I always complete the two monthly expectations for the ends of month one and two. However, I only write out the weekly expectations for the first month to simplify the process. If you desire to write all 12 of the weekly outlooks, you may choose to do so!

Breakdown of your weekly time blocks

For each week, you are required to fulfill seven time blocks, which means you could commit to one block a day each day and complete the requirements that you need. Overall, these time blocks, when added together, will provide you with six hours towards your S.M.A.R.T. outcome. Now before you say, "I don't have an extra six hours in my week," don't fret. My bonus module in *time management* will free up more than enough time for you to apply towards your outcome!

Simply go to:

https://www.docdeliversbooks.com/free-ebook/

and scroll down to the section called "Time Management Module."

Here are your required time blocks:

"The Time Efficient 25"

"The Magic 60"

"The One Time 120"

"The Time Efficient 25"

This is based off the Pomodoro Technique which again is focusing on working without distraction for 25 minutes, followed by a five-minute break to allow for you to mentally recharge.

It is a simplified version of the Pomodoro Technique because in the extended version, it would involve cycles of 25 minutes, followed by five minutes of rest, after which the cycle repeats, up to two hours.

For your week, you will be required to schedule in **four blocks** of this time frame, placing and utilizing them as they best fit your schedule and outcome, respectively.

"The Magic 60"

This time frame is simply two Pomodoro blocks, connected with a five-minute rest break in between, thus you would have a 25-minute block, followed by five minutes of rest, a second 25-minute block which again is followed by five minutes of rest.

For your week, you will be required to schedule in **two blocks** of this time frame, placing and utilizing them as they best fit your schedule and outcome, respectively.

"The One Time 120"

This time frame is simply four Pomodoro blocks, connected by five-minute rest breaks, thus every ½ hour during the two-hour time block, you are completing one 25-minute Pomodoro block followed by five minutes of rest.

For your week, you will be required to schedule in **one block** of the One-Time 120, placing and utilizing it as it best fits your schedule and outcome, respectively.

Combined, these seven time blocks represent six hours that will be applied towards your S.M.A.R.T. outcome. Again, the bonus module on time management will help you free up more than enough time to achieve this. So, you may ask, "Where do I put the time blocks at throughout my week?"

That, my friend, is totally up to do!

I have allowed you the flexibility to create your own schedule.

You could choose to have one time block a day for 6 of the seven days and be complete.

You could choose to do multiple time blocks, such as the longer two-hour time block on a weekend morning and a shorter 25-minute one later that day.

So, in summary, you will have the following 7 time blocks:

4 blocks of "The Time Efficient 25"

2 blocks of "The Magic 60"

1 block of "The One-Time 120"

The key is assisting you with developing a pattern where you do a minimum of six hours of work a week, because after 90 days of doing it, it will become an automatic pattern for you.

The six hours of time blocks are a *minimum* because I, and many of my clients that I coach, understand the power of getting a massive amount of work done with undistracted and focused concentration. You could choose to add more time and to do this, simply add an extra "Time Efficient 25," "Magic 60," or "One-Time 120" towards your schedule.

Let's make sure you truly understand the time blocks. These are times with ZERO distractions.

No TV or music playing in the background, no internet (unless your time block requires it), no phone, no disruptions.

Absolute silence and no distractions. If you haven't experienced doing a Pomodoro time block, you will be pleasantly surprised just how much work you can and will get done in only 25 minutes. But ONLY if it is without interruptions or distractions.

Daily actions and nightly reflections

Each day, in your personal journal, or utilizing the 90-day journal that I have created and you can purchase, you will mark down which time block(s) that you will complete for the day. If you have the journal, simply circle the specific one that you commit to. These time blocks will correspond to the S.M.A.R.T. outcome that you desire, either:

Your Personal Self

Your Social Self

Your Financial Self

If you haven't purchased my 90-Day Outcome Journal, here are some sample sheets to help you get started. Check out:

https://www.docdeliversbooks.com/free-ebook/

and scroll down to the section called "Sample 90-Day Outcome Journal Sheets."

On this page, you can also purchase the journal.

For now, I encourage you to start with ONE S.M.A.R.T. outcome for your first 90-day run. It's critical for you to get through the first 90 days without getting overwhelmed or frustrated because if that happens, your likelihood of quitting skyrockets and we definitely don't want that! I say this because for each S.M.A.R.T. outcome, it's going to potentially require extra time. So, if you decide to tackle two of them, you may be looking at 12 hours of time blocks during the week instead of six. If you do all three outcomes, now it's potentially 18 hours for the week. Again, I will help you find the time that you need through the "time management" bonus module but there is no need to overwhelm you from day one. You potentially could do all three outcomes with just 12 hours of weekly time block commitments and you probably will be able to do so after developing the necessary habits, discipline, and efficiency that you will gain from the first 90-day run with just one S.MA.R.T. outcome.

After determining your time block for the day, you then will fill out the outcome that you desire for it. Next, circle **"the one"** action that you will complete. If you are doing just one S.M.A.R.T. outcome, then this may be the only one you have on your sheet. If you have more than one

S.M.A.R.T. outcome for the day, circling the one action that you commit to will remind you of which one of the two (or three) are critical for the day.

After completing this, there is a very important step which will frame your day in a positive way. *Writing down your gratitude statements.* Gratitude is essential in my life and has helped me achieve far more than I could have ever imagined! It doesn't have to be hard because you are just writing three things that you are currently grateful for. I write 10 every day so three is easy peasy! This can be as simple as saying, "I'm grateful for my family," or "I'm grateful for being alive today," or "I'm grateful for my job today."

When you are grateful for what you have, the doors of opportunity open for you because how would you ever expect to get more money, happiness, health, and wealth if you are not grateful for what you have now? Think about it.

Finally, for the daily action sheet, you will write a simple optimistic thought for the day. It could be your list of three to five core values. For example, I would write, "today, I am a determined, disciplined, and unstoppable man." It could be a power statement from your C.A.L.M.I.N.G. statements that you learned in the F.E.A.R. module of your second trimester. Here are the examples again of those statements:

"I'm **C**onfident that I can...."

"I take **A**ction today to get closer to the outcomes tomorrow."

"**L**ife becomes more exciting as I grow out of my fear."

"**M**emories of success are within me."

"**I** can do anything for…"

"**N**ow is the time to act."

"**G**rowth is what I strive for, each and every day."

In your "night reflections," we go back to the days of the good ole Wild West and reflect upon "The Good, The Bad, and The Ugly."

Instead of ugly, because it's so negative, we will use 02E or your "opportunity to excel."

The good are the positives or victories that have been achieved during the day. Celebrate the wins whenever they come!

The bad are the things that didn't go so well for you and that's ok. Remember, these are learning opportunities that you will expand upon in the final section, your 02E.

Your 02E is your opportunity to further reflect and expand upon what didn't work out so well and some possible solutions to minimizing or eliminating it in the future.

Next, you check off the time blocks that you completed that day. Sounds simple but writing down and seeing this adds up, building the momentum of locking in a habit of doing daily time blocks.

At night, I love to reflect because it's a quiet time for me and my mind is usually clear. Here, I brainstorm upon the potential actions that I desire for the next day. This is the opportunity to write them down. Often, I skip writing down the actions on the night reflections and instantly document them on the next day's daily action sheet. This way, I already have a head start on the next day. For me personally, my morning time before 11 am is where I get much of my work done, so having the actions already planned out for the day is huge for me. Finally, I leave a section to record any additional thoughts that you may have. Feel free to use, or not use this section as you best see fit.

To optimize your morning and evening journaling, I have included a second bonus module for you for free. It is my personal morning and evening ritual strategy and it's my pleasure to share it with you.

You may download this by going to:

https://www.docdeliversbooks.com/free-ebook/

and scroll down to the section called "Daily and Evening Rituals."

90-day outcome, monthly expectations, and weekly review sheets

The 90-day Outcome Journal sheet is where you will write down your outcomes, Your Social Life, Your Personal Life, or Your Financial Life outcomes. Remember, start with one for the first 90-day cycle. Also included on this sheet is a section to record your "core values" and "my why." Your seven level deep "why" statements get to the core of why you wish to deliver an enhanced version of you! I feel it's important to document this because you can open your journal and instantly see your why and values, especially important during the rough patches that you will encounter. Again, there are samples at:

https://www.docdeliversbooks.com/free-ebook/

and scroll down to the section called "Sample 90-Day Outcome Journal Sheets."

We previously talked about the **monthly expectations**, which are your 90-day S.M.A.R.T. outcomes broken down into 28- and 56-day checkpoints. On this sheet, your month one and two targets will be established, breaking down the 90-day outcome, which could be overwhelming or intimidating, into smaller components. Do you know how to eat an elephant? One bite at a time!

In the **monthly review** sheets, you will review if you did or didn't hit your expectation targets for your desired outcome(s). If not, reflect upon the past month and determine why that was the case. This is also a checkpoint for seeing what you can do better for the upcoming month, even if you completed your expectations. Always look for the opportunity to grow. Finally, there is a section to record any reflections that you have for the month.

The **weekly preview** sheets are designed to further breakdown the monthly expectations into even more manageable waypoints towards your overall outcome. Simply document the weekly outlooks that you commit to for your specific outcome. Take the time to stop and reflect upon your monthly expectation, making sure your weekly actions are moving you towards them and you are not simply filling your day with "stuff." Your outcome is not to be "**busy**" with filler stuff, things that make you feel and look busy but have no impact upon your monthly expectation or 90-day S.M.A.R.T. outcome. Your outcome is to be "**productive**."

With that being said, you will write down the "time vampires" that you will slay. These are the things like television, useless web browsing, or social media channel engagement, which may be fun to do, but suck the life and time out of your day. The "Time Management" bonus module goes more into this.

Write down one that you will tackle or eliminate for the week. Finally, you have the space to write down any thoughts that you have for the upcoming week. Use this section as you best see fit!

Finally, let's breakdown the **week in review**. Here, you will document whether you achieved your personal, social, and financial outlooks for the week. If so, wonderful. If not, wonderful! You have a great learning opportunity to see how to make this outcome better, brainstorming on ways to minimize or eliminate the thing or things that caused you to fall short of the target. Outside of this, if there are any other things that you feel you can improve upon for the week, write them down on the sheet. There is a spot just for this! Finally, you have the opportunity to reflect upon the week and share your thoughts with yourself and your worksheet!

Each day, locking in "the one" …

Since, you have seven time blocks that you will commit to each week, most likely you will do one per day. To help facilitate your success for the week, think of these blocks as the absolutes that are to be completed no matter what. It is typically the most important task that you must complete and because of this, stress its importance and make the commitment to complete it. Will your S.M.A.R.T. outcomes totally collapse if you don't lock in and complete **the one**?

Absolutely not. However, going through the 90 days, continually not doing this will lock in a pattern, a habit that you don't want: complacency. Yes, there will be days when life overwhelms you or you are at the end of the day and your one is not complete. Suck it up and do it! You may think that one day is not going to drastically change your life, but it can. What if you failed to make that needed call to a client, the one who introduced you to someone who significantly brings your business to the next level? What if you decided to skip the gym today and, on that day, your partner who was meant for you would have been on the treadmill beside you?

You just never know.

Am I excited *each and every day* I wake up at 4:45 am to start my workouts? Hell no! Some days it sucks, and I think of every excuse not to do it, but I still push through it. Challenge yourself to grow to the next level, striving to get a little better every day. Believe me when I tell you this, when you complete the 90 days, those things that you previously thought as major obstacles will just be miniscule speedbumps along your journey.

So, as you progress through your day, understand that there is the one that must be completed. Within your "daily actions" sheet, you will mark or circle "the one" action that is the most important of the day. And as you complete the day and complete your nightly reflection, you will answer, simply yes or no, if you are D.O.N.E. today or in other words:

Did One Necessary Event today (D.O.N.E.). This is **the one** that you need to complete for the day, no matter what. Often it is the most challenging thing you will do. Once this one is done, you will find that your other outcomes are easier and less stressful.

If you say no, don't look upon it as a bad thing! It's simply a reflection of what didn't work today, providing you the opportunity to improve upon it. I grow and learn so much more from my failures than my successes that I treasure the opportunity to dissect out the issue and strive to set the plan that will minimize it from happening again.

Again, feel free to download the journal sample pages to get started by going to:

https://www.docdeliversbooks.com/free-ebook/

and scroll down to the section called "Sample 90 Day Journal Outcome Sheets."

Taking the R.I.G.H.T. Action and developing habits

Let's go and take the R.I.G.H.T. Action!

This was first introduced in your second trimester, so I will briefly reflect upon it. It served you well to take the actions necessary to overcome your F.E.A.R. and will serve you again as you begin your 90-day journey. Remember the R.I.G.H.T. Action:

The R.I.G.H.T. Action

R – resilient

I – instantaneous

G – grateful

H – harmonious

T – time efficient

Resilient action is that action you continue to take, despite the challenges, obstacles, or setbacks. Basically, keep moving forward and don't quit!

Instantaneous action is what happens now. Don't overthink the situation, just move forward and take the necessary action.

Grateful action is reflecting upon the action that you have taken, being grateful for your courage to strive forward and being grateful for what you have now, opening the doors to get more of what you strive for.

Harmonious action is action which is consistent with your why. Being congruent with why you wish to develop an enhanced version of you and having actions that support that is a beautiful thing!

Time efficient action is action that favors quality over quantity, while simultaneously doing the maximum amount of action in the minimum amount of time.

The process of making your actions a habit

Here is a great way to understand the power of developing habits, a concept that has been in the world of psychology for many years and enhanced by Charles Duhigg's bestselling book, "The Power of Habit." James Clear, author of "Atomic Habits," made Duhigg's three step pattern of cue, routine, and reward more memorable with his 3R's concept of reminder, routine, and reward.

Reminder

Let's take the example of having a S.M.A.R.T. outcome of losing 20 pounds in 90 days. The *reminder* is the physical trigger that reminds you to do so. For example, for this outcome, the trigger could be having a glass of water and an apple on the counter by your car keys, reminding you each morning to hydrate and eat healthy. Your triggers can either be events that you create or things that you do daily that you can link with the outcome. These pre-existing triggers could be things like setting your home alarm each day, listening to a song in your car on your way to work or leaving work each day. You could link these events with triggers such as a sticky note on the alarm encouraging you to work out or creating a prerecorded audio for your car with a prerecorded message that automatically plays when you turn on your ignition. Have fun with this and see how you can create links and triggers that will serve you best!

Routine

Routine is about taking small steps with your actions. Going from the couch potato and sedentary life towards deciding you want to run five miles the next day probably won't work! Not only is it going to hurt physically, mentally it could crush you and do the opposite, which is never wanting to run again. So, start small and do actions that are effective and repeatable. It's not about taking massive action. It's about taking action that will be repeatable and sustainable. Trust me, you want to be the person who starts small and hits the outcome rather than the one who takes massive action and burns out by day 17.

Reward

Celebration is not just critical, it's just outright fun! I don't care if you ate junk food all your life and on day one, you ate two apples. It doesn't matter if you were shy all your life and you took the initiative to talk with a stranger for 30 seconds. *Reward* these times because they are victories for you. I simply don't understand why some people won't give themselves credit until they hit their endpoint or target. That simply doesn't make sense! Enjoy the victories along the way because you are stacking them, creating momentum that will fuel you as you continue the journey.

As you progress through your 90 days, remember to set your triggers for your outcomes (reminder), take the small action steps that will sustain you (routine) and celebrate your wins along the way (reward)!

Your next 90 days...

This is it! Finally, you have arrived at the stage in your rebirth that you take that first act, that first step towards your S.M.A.R.T. outcome. For getting to this stage in your journey, I must say congratulations to you! If you have your journal, mark down this date as the first day of your journey towards an enhanced version of you. If not, mark it down somewhere, because in 90 days from now, after the victories and setbacks, you will be exactly where you need to be. Most likely, it's the point of achieving your S.M.A.R.T. outcome(s). For others, you may fall short of the outcome but still have excitement and celebrate the fact that you took the journey. Most people will continue to live in their comfort loops, never understanding, desiring, or having the ability to overcome the fear to either stretch or break it.

Fortunately, that's not you and if you have any doubts about it, don't!

Do you know that many people don't pass the first three chapters of a book? Look at where you are now. You have a solid preconception foundation with your seven level deep why and have redefined your limiting beliefs. Your journey through the Circle of Conception has strengthened your core with solid values, strategies, and techniques for overcoming your fears and obstacles, and powerful visualization techniques to see your success right now!

You are ready for your transformation, ready to start the first day of the next 90, a journey that will vastly improve your life!

Say to yourself now, "Thank you for the journey that I have taken, and I am grateful for having the strength, courage and determination to begin it." You are worth it because you are moving forward in ways that will integrate with your subconscious, making the journey more natural and automatic as you proceed with it.

Now remember, many people will not do what you are doing, making the effort to conceive your dreams, overcome your fears and obstacles and deliver an enhanced version of you. Many people won't take this journey because they don't understand they are still stuck in their comfort loops. And what people don't understand, they may question, fear, or outright reject. Know in advance that those who you may think support you and have your back may not. That's ok because the haters out there are a good thing! Personally, I love the haters because it's my feedback to let me know I am stretching myself, living beyond my own comfort loop and growing. You need the haters because they will be a part of your measuring stick, letting you know you are indeed changing beyond their visual perceptions of the previous version of you.

Don't hate the haters, embrace them.

They will be the people who come to you as your success and growth continues, wanting to gain enlightenment on how your transformation can help guide them along a transformation that they desire. I always believed that life is not just about helping yourself, you grow even more when you help those behind you! Don't ever forget that.

So today, not only do I want you to congratulate yourself but also make the verbal commitment to complete your 90-day journey, despite the obstacles, challenges, and setbacks that you will encounter. Setbacks happen to everyone, but you are now equipped with the tools to overcome them!

Get up right now, stand confidently and say to yourself today:

"I, state your name, commit to the next 90 days despite the challenges and setbacks, because when I complete my outcome, I will have vastly improved my life and as I reflect upon the completion of my journey at the end of my 90 days, I will know that all of my success and accomplishments will be a reflection of the small yet powerful commitment that I made today."

As you move forward, don't think of this book and your journey as linear. You have been presented so many nuggets, techniques, and strategies that will serve you well. So, if you feel the need to reflect upon previous stages of your development, either the preconception care or Circle of Conception, do it! My desire for you is to help create the mindset that your growth is a never-ending journey. Once you hit your S.M.A.R.T. outcomes, that's not the end of your journey. It's a new beginning because it's the opportunity to reflect upon and grow yourself to the next level.

With that being said, you are now at level three, your postconceptional care and the final stage of your development (for now!)

Here, you develop a mindset of F.R.E.E.D.O.M. and reflect upon what you "HAVE."

SECTION 4

Level 3: Freedom

Chapter 12

Level three concludes with defining what you HAVE. It is within the Circle of Conception and represents its conclusion, however, the power of having what you want is so strong, that I felt it deserved a level and section of its own. It is the natural transition point from flowing in and out of your Circle of Conception and moving towards your future developmental growth. It also serves as the bridge for continuing your journey because HAVE is not an end point, it is simply the beginning. Life is not linear, it's a continuous circle of growth. Think about it like what you have in life serving as a foundation before continuing your developmental journey and evaluating what you possess. Not necessarily material possessions but emotional, physical, mental, and spiritual ones. Once you see what you have, it's time to decide to stay within your comfort loop or take the next step to expand or break it. Either one of the latter choices will reset the cycle, having you reevaluate and possibly redefine your why, bringing your growth back towards level one and your preconception care.

Life is a circle, with continuous growth, continuous reevaluation of who you are, where you are, why you are there and what decision needs to be made next. The choice is this:

Do I stay comfortable for a while and absorb what I have achieved or accomplished, or do I expand or break my comfort loop and move towards the next level?

Understanding where you are, what you HAVE, will help answer this question for you.

So, what does this have to do with freedom? Excellent question and we will dive into that right now. Freedom is the main theme of this level and as you continue to read this section, absorbing the material and listening to my words, you will begin to realize that having a mindset ***now*** of being free as opposed to striving for it in the ***future*** will vastly improve your life.

What is F.R.E.E.D.O.M.?

So, what is F.R.E.E.D.O.M.? You will later understand the mnemonic, but for now, let's focus on the word itself, freedom? What is it? Is freedom something imposed on one individual or group towards another? Or is it a mindset?

Ask yourself this very important question and take the time to answer it honestly.

Am I free?

Go beyond the physical nine to five job you may have or your financial situation or your personal relationships. Think of the question mentally, dig deeper, and ask yourself again:

Are you free?

It's really a tough question for some, especially if you haven't thought of it this way. The reason why I ask you this question is because it blows my mind when people say one of their goals in life is to be free.

Free from what?!?! Free from your boss, your bills, bad relationships, bloated physique?

Because you may be in one or these situations or a similar one, do you still think you are not free?

The point is, you are already free. You may think that physical aspects of your life hold you back from being free but that's not the truth. It's a cop out, a lie that you have told to yourself, engrained within your subconscious, and used as a pity-party excuse to make you feel better about yourself. Yes, I understand you wish to ease the pain but there is a better and far superior way to do.it.

Instead of thinking of freedom as a physical or tangible aspect of your life, think of it as a mental one. Mentally, you are FREE to move away from your circumstances, to break or expand the comfort loop that holds you in your life where you are now.

You, and only you, are the thing that keeps you from being and feeling free.

Not your boss, your job, your finances, or relationships.

You!

Let's get back to defining F.R.E.E.D.O.M.

When the times come, and they will, that setbacks happen (and they always do, for everybody) reflect on this mnemonic, which will remind you of who you are, what you are striving for, and why you are taking this wonderful journey in the first place:

*F*ree your mind of the shackles that hold it back

*R*elease your fears

*E*mbrace your greatness and stay grateful

*E*levate your actions and keep pushing to the next level

*D*etermine your new outcomes in life

*O*pen your mind to grow even further, having what you desire

*M*ove to enlighten the people who follow you

Write this down and place it in a spot where you will see it every day. It's going to be your trigger that will help keep you pushing forward, remembering the bigger picture.

Each of these subtly touches upon all the levels of your developmental growth, from your preconception care all the way to level three, the freedom to have what you desire.

Remember, freedom is a state of mind, with you having the power to choose your level of freedom because you, and only you, control it. Making the choice to rise above your circumstances and choose to enhance your life in significant ways is the ultimate level of freedom. Being free is the beginning, a powerful start towards your new mindset where you initiate the strength and courage to unshackle your mind, conceive your ideas, and develop yourself in order to deliver an enhanced version of you!

You "have" what you desire, how do you "have" more?

Again, congratulations for reaching this stage in your development! From your initial preconception development towards your rebirth and taking the actions necessary to achieve your S.M.A.R.T. outcomes, you have or are beginning to have the things that you desire. And that could be any number of things, mentally, physically, spiritually, or emotionally. Things such as having more happiness, connection with a higher power, physical fitness, financial gain, deeper or enhanced relationships. The list goes on and on. You have empowered yourself with tools and techniques, allowing yourself to strive for your outcomes, having the things that you desire. You accomplished this by either stretching or breaking your existing comfort loop, transitioning to a new level of comfort. And when I say a new level of comfort, that is not implying anything negative, it simply means you have grown beyond the self-limiting loop that you have placed yourself in and upgraded to a bigger one!

Now what?

You may decide that this new comfort loop is perfect for your life and you wish to stay in this loop for a time that you desire. On the other hand, your personal growth has awakened a hunger within you, hungry for more in your life and a desire to grow even further. You want more, but two questions must be asked first?

What exactly do I **have** now?

What do I want to **have** in the future?

Knowing what you have now is the first step towards determining what you desire to have in the future.

One of the first ways to do this is to reflect upon your original set of core values. For example, you may have core values of **determination,**

discipline, and congruency. As you near completion of your 90-day S.M.A.R.T. outcome journey (or even better, after completing it), ask yourself this:

Did my outcomes bring me closer towards my defined core values?

Let's say your outcome was losing 20 pounds in a 90-day period and you achieved the outcome. Yes, you hit the target, so the next step is to reflect upon your core values. You begin the internal dialogue with yourself, asking, "As I progressed through the 90 days, was I **determined** each day to succeed no matter what? Did I exercise **discipline** with my choices with exercise and diet? Was I **congruent** in leading by example, telling others of the importance of a proper diet and practicing what I preached?"

Your 90-day process is not meant to be a simple task of having a beginning and an end. It is meant to be an educational journey for yourself, evaluating your progress mentally, emotionally, physically, and spiritually to educate yourself on what works, what doesn't work and how you can grow even further. As you reflect upon the 90 days, you evaluate to see if you have grown into the core values that you desired at the start. If you have, feeling that the outcome has created a habit of, shall we say, discipline, because you worked out and stayed compliant with your meal plan during that time, then you have successfully integrated that core value as a habit. And once your core value is a habit for you, it becomes more natural to express that core value without a second thought. On the other hand, you can still achieve the outcome yet not grow into the core value as deeply as you desired.

No worries, because this is the first question, "What do I have now?"

Knowing what you have now, in this case the integration of your core values, will let you know if you feel that your journey has moved you towards them in the way that you desired or is there room to grow even more.

That opens you up for the second question, "What do I want to have in the future?"

You could desire to have more discipline in our example, especially if you felt that you needed to tighten up your compliance with diet and exercise. Or you may decide that all three of your core values of discipline, determination, and congruency were significantly enhanced during your 90-day journey. You may wish to add an additional core value, strengthen an existing one even more, or replace a core value that is so integrated as an internal habit, that replacing it in your mental list will cause no loss for you.

The key is this:

Understand what your core values are and if you are satisfied with the growth of them. Think of your core values as unwritten outcomes that parallel your 90-day journey. Growing into your self-defined core value is just as important (or in some cases, even more important) than the S.M.A.R.T. outcomes themselves.

So, own it, and begin to develop the mindset that you have freedom NOW because you have the power to take action and move away from your current circumstances and towards outcomes that better serve you. You may say, "Well that's easy to say and hard to do." No, it's not! Another cop-out excuse that you and others may make because you are comfortable within your loop, empowered with millions of years of evolutionary development in the form of your fight or flight response which keeps you safe and seeks to avoid you going through pain. What pain? The pain of possible failure, rejection, setbacks, defeats, which people may encounter as they try to change their circumstances.

It's not hard to do because it only takes the first step to get the momentum going. I didn't say a massive leap, but just one simple step, one initial action that moves you towards the outcomes that you desire.

Your only shackles in life are self-imposed so release them, embrace the freedom that you already have and mentally accept it!

Freedom is not feeling physically trapped, it's the mental choice to act and decide to change your life for the better. Given the fact that you picked up this book and read damn near all of it tells me you have already embraced freedom, maybe not on a conscious level but at least subconsciously because you are taking the steps to enhance your life, to deliver an enhanced version of yourself!

How Does This Relate to HAVE?

Freedom is understanding the choice to HAVE what your desire in life. Reflect upon your developmental growth so far. You made the choice to BE more, redefining your core beliefs and values, DO the things that were essential to overcome your fears and obstacles, SEE your brighter future through powerful visualization techniques, ACT with precision, power, and passion to move you closer to your outcomes, and in time, you will achieve them and HAVE what you desire and deserve in life.

What do you wish to have as you complete your 90-day journey towards your outcomes? Part of it is within your why statements, another component may incorporate your core values. Understand that once you have what you desire, it's not the end of the journey for you, it is simply the beginning.

But it's only the beginning if you choose it to be, and you have the freedom to make that choice.

You have the freedom to accept what you have now, as you progress towards or complete your 90-day S.M.A.R.T. outcome(s) or grow beyond them.

There is nothing wrong with the choice to take a step back and appreciate what you have and savor the moment of your accomplishments. I encourage you to do so. What is wrong is staying within your comfort loop and growing complacent. It's a step backwards when you decide, "I don't need or desire anymore and I'm fine here." I am a firm believer that people never stop evolving, unless they choose to.

So, I challenge you, when you are ready to do so, to make the choice to keep developing and keep growing. You have the freedom to play small after your first 90-day S.M.A.R.T. outcome round or play a bigger game.

The bigger game is...

Remember how I told you I wanted you to focus on just one S.M.A.R.T. outcome during your first 90 days? The reason is because I wanted you to take the first 90 days and use it not only for achieving your S.M.A.R.T. outcomes but more importantly, developing habits that will become automatic for you, making you more efficient, consistent, and effective with achieving your daily actions, weekly goals, and monthly expectations.

Unless you are a really slow reader, chances are you are finishing up this book before hitting the 90-day mark so think of this as future preparation and planning for the next 90 days. "What, I have to do another cycle?" Yep, if you wish to keep developing and that's the whole purpose of this journey, isn't it? I have NO doubts that you will do it because as you approach your 90 days and complete it, you are going to be begging for more because the vast improvements in your life will keep you going!

As you move, starting to prepare for the second round of your 90-day S.M.A.R.T. outcome cycle, it's time to take off the training wheels! By this time, your skills with time management, taking R.I.G.H.T. Action and having the habits to consistently complete your actions daily will have provided you with the tools which are necessary for expanding your comfort loop (or quite possibly breaking it)!

Now, you only have to worry about three outcomes and the reason for accomplishing all three is for obtaining balance in your life. Think of a three-legged stool and when you take away one leg, the stool falls over. That's like your life. Focus on the personal and the social selves and the financial one falters. Put all of your efforts towards financial growth and your personal and relationship growth falls off. The key is to strive for harmony with all three legs or outcomes. How do you do this, you may ask? By NOT trying to accomplish actions for all three outcomes on the same day. Decide what is "your one" for the day and put all your mental and physical energy towards that action. Trying to flip between two or three outcomes in the same day may be challenging. Not saying it can't be done. My task is to guide and mentor you on your path and I wish to avoid you overloading yourself on any given day, leading to mental burnout and leaving your outcomes on the side of the road.

So, for example, you could decide to have three S.M.A.R.T. outcomes for 90 days such as:

Personal – "In 90 days, on July 22nd, 2018, I will have lost 20 pounds in weight."

Social – "In 90 days, on July 22nd, 2018, I will have completed the "Love Dare" challenge with my spouse."

Financial – "In 90 days, on July 22nd, 2018, I will raise $500 for charity by running in a local charity's 5K run on July 14th, 2018."

The sky is the limit for you. These are not overwhelmingly hard outcomes, just a template for you to work with. Follow the S.M.A.R.T. technique and choose outcomes that will stretch you and are well defined. In time, you will continue to stretch and eventually break your comfort loops as you set new foundations for yourself and the outcomes become more challenging. That is what growth is all about!

Knowing what you have now is the first step to having more

You may ask, "Does this mean that what I have should always be a reflection of my core values?"

Absolutely not!

I only used the core values as a teaching point so that you can understand the concept of the two important questions:

What exactly do I have now?

What do I want to have in the future?

During your 90-day journey, you may have discovered something that you wish to have that you would incorporate into your next round of S.M.A.R.T. outcomes. For example, you may have had the internal outcome of weight loss but discovered during your progress that you desired a deeper connection with your family, wanting them to be healthy and fit like you. Your next S.M.A.R.T. outcome could be "I will have an hour family fitness day each Saturday for the next 90 days, where I focus on family and no work-related events."

Or, discovering what you wanted to have next may have nothing to do with the core values or outcomes themselves. It could have been a random observation or thought during the journey. Again, reflection upon your 90-day journey will give you insight into where you are and where you want to go for your continuing journey.

What do I have *now* and what do I want to have *more of in my future*?

Another way to look at and discover what you wish to have more of would be asking these three powerful questions after completing your 90-day S.M.A.R.T. outcome cycle. Yes, I love asking questions and as you continue to read the words, absorb this information, and discover what you have, you will begin to realize that asking yourself questions is the ultimate way to be real with yourself and do a thorough self-analysis. You have asked yourself these questions every day during your 90-day journey, so this would serve as a simple reminder for you:

What was good about my overall 90-day journey?

What was bad about my overall 90-day journey?

What could I have improved upon within my 90-day journey to make it even better?

After completing your 90-day journey, these are the final questions that you would ask yourself, providing you with a powerful self-reflection and analysis.

The "duality of have" and going back to the beginning of your development

Once you know what you have now and desire to have more in the future, then the next step is going back to level one of the process, your foundation and preconception care. Think of it not as starting over but enhancing what you already have. Life is a continuous loop of growth, one where you are constantly growing and challenging yourself to reach the next level in your development. Going back to your preconception care is your trigger for being excited about what you know and have now, going through the process again so that you can have even more of what you desire and deserve in life.

And before you begin the next round of your developmental growth, take a moment to reflect upon what you have. Embrace what you have achieved because you have worked hard for it! Take pride in the fact that you rose to the challenge. Let's reflect upon your journey, shall we!

You destroyed and redefined your limiting beliefs, understanding, and appreciating what was possible in your future.

You defined a powerful "why," providing you with an overall purpose for any outcome that you choose.

You identified your core values, knowing the person that you wished to BE.

You determined what to mentally DO with the fears that you have, overcoming them and moving forward towards your desired outcomes.

You learned how to SEE your success now, despite the outcomes being future events, building the confidence for your subsequent actions.

You learned how to physically ACT and get in the game, taking the steps necessary for achieving your outcomes.

You achieved what you wanted to HAVE, realizing this was just the first step in this amazing journey, which has vastly improved your life.

Congratulations to you!

Most people do not and will not do what you have done. Being near the end of the book is an accomplishment, given that so many people start one and don't even complete it. Your journey along your development towards an enhanced version of yourself may have been paved with setbacks, defeats, and failures; however, your persistence to grow reflects your drive and determination to move beyond your comfort loop, moving to a bigger and better you.

What is even more exciting is the possibility of your actions rubbing off on others. Family, friends, loved ones, coworkers, and acquaintances have been there to witness your transformation and seeing accomplishments in others is inspiring to watch! Basically, you released the limitations that held you back, took life by the horns and steered towards the outcomes that best served you.

Embrace this moment, knowing that you have vastly improved your life!

The Duality of HAVE

Here is the duality of having what you want. Appreciate and embrace what you have achieved but don't suffocate it!

The duality is **accepting what you have** and **letting it go** at the same time.

One of the dangers of having what you desired is that it overwhelms you. One of two things can happen. You may be overexcited from what you gained and begin *losing focus* on where you are at. Or, you get so excited that it brings you to a level where you get cocky, *losing appreciation* of what you have gained.

So, how do you avoid losing focus or appreciation of what you have?

You let it go.

And by letting it go, you are not diminishing its value or importance in anyway. You are acknowledging that you have the discipline to care enough not to care (as my mentor would say!) It's important to you but not so much that it causes a loss. Think of it this way. You are house training your small puppy by having them in a crate intermittently throughout the day. Eventually, as they learn and appreciate their freedom, they learn how not to have accidents because the negative consequence could land them back in the cage and inhibit their freedom. You learn to trust your pet, appreciating them for learning not to have accidents in the cage, rewarding their trust by letting them roam free, in time.

Learn to trust yourself and appreciate what you have gained. Care about it enough to have appreciation and trust in the fact that you can appreciate what you have gained and let it go at the same time.

The power in the duality of what you have, allowing you to simultaneously appreciate and let go of what you have after you complete your S.M.A.R.T. outcomes, will allow you not to get too complacent or overexcited. Basically, you are in a neutral position of gratitude, not too little, not too much. Why is this important? Because both sides of the equation are necessary. Excessively being grateful all the time for what you have doesn't allow you to trust in yourself, knowing that you have the power to retain what you have gained without losing it. Not letting go of what you have and not being grateful may cause you to lose your focus and appreciation of it. You have mentally diminished the value of what you have, losing out on the benefits that you have gained.

Like night and day, or the sun and moon, one doesn't exist without the other.

Having more if you are still unsure of what you want to have…

Sometimes, despite using your core values as a guide or reflecting upon your 90-day journey, you still may tell yourself, "I still don't know what I want to have more of." There is an additional technique that you can do if you still feel stuck.

If you are unsure of what you want more of, try to focus on what you don't want. Reflect upon your journey and as you ask yourself the question, "What was bad about my 90-day journey?" Sometimes it can be far easier to think about the negative of a situation. Now understand, I typically wouldn't want you to focus on the negative because much of the time, it can be self-defeating. However, in this case, it will serve you well. Let's use our trusty example again of losing 20 pounds in 90 days and you achieved the outcome during your defined time. However, you are not sure what you would want more of. You may feel that your weight is ideal now and you have the dietary and exercise habits that you desire. Well, on the surface, you may struggle to figure out what you have more of because everything appears complete. Now is the time you ask yourself, "What was bad about the 90-day journey?" Using this powerful question, you may mentally reflect or review on your nightly reflection notes that there were days in the week that you didn't have the dietary compliance that you desired. The weight gain was achieved, however, there were more "cheat days" than you originally planned for. This self-reflection revealed that there were times you were undisciplined.

For the upcoming exercise, "Having More When You Are Stuck," you can download the worksheet at:

https://www.docdeliversbooks.com/free-ebook/

The purpose of this exercise is to see what was bad, what didn't work, and then looking at the opposite effect. In our case, this would represent having more discipline with your diet and thus, could be something that you would want to have more of. Make it simple for yourself and pull out your worksheet. If you don't have the worksheet, simply get a piece of paper, and draw a line down the middle from top to bottom. On the left side, write down the things that were bad and didn't work out the way you desired during your 90-day outcome journey. On the other side, in the right column, write down the opposite outcome, building a nice list that you can reference and analyze to see if there are things that you would like to have more of.

Between reanalyzing your core values, reflecting upon your 90-day outcome journey, and physically writing down a list of what didn't work for you (with its associated opposites), you have three tools at your disposal that will serve you well. The key is understanding and determining what you want to have more of, continuing your growth of delivering an even more enhanced version of yourself with your next 90-day outcome journey.

Taking your developmental growth to the next level

There will be times where you have an outcome in mind that is so powerful and challenging, it could require more than you are physically or mentally capable of doing. The greater the success, vision, dream, or idea, the greater the need for a strong support system. Some people are capable thinkers and doers, who may be challenged but are more than capable of going for it on their own. However, there are people who have outcomes that are beyond the norm, ideas and outcomes that are remarkable, phenomenally altering their lives, and quite possibly their community and world around them... that requires teamwork and the support of others.

It can be hard to move onto your next level of development when you don't feel like you're strong enough to carry any more weight. Here's where having an amazing circle of influence comes in!

The first distinction you'll want to understand about creating the right mastermind group is accountability and support. Having a circle of influence that holds you accountable to do the things you want. A circle that will help you better yourself and support you through the times you get burned out, frustrated, or simply stuck from moving forward.

A properly selected mastermind group is constantly pulling, pushing, encouraging, challenging, supporting, and loving you, never giving up on each other or saying you should quit. That's what you need your group to provide. More importantly, that's also what you should aspire to provide to others because the more you give of yourself to others, the greater you will receive in turn.

The second distinction is summed up nicely within a few sayings you've heard before. Birds of a feather flock together…like attracts like…water seeks its own level.

All these sayings refer to a similar concept that simply says you will gravitate towards, attract, make friends with, find things in common with and spend time with those who are like you on some level in life.

When creating your mastermind group, you reflect upon the entry point of your Circle of Conception, specifically your first trimester. Who do you desire to BE in the world? Evaluate the people in your current circle of influence. Those who you spend the majority of your time with. Ask yourself the tough question, "Are they helping or distracting you from your growth and progress?" The question is tough because this could be close family members or friends who you may not want to offend or upset. Pay attention because this is critical! *You cannot let anybody hold you back once you are committed.* It can be hard to cut the ties that you need to and if this is done, do the work on yourself and then return to share the knowledge and help those who were holding you back. I didn't say it would be easy to do. You have the freedom to decide whether you want to stay within your comfort loop surrounded by the people who don't serve you or would you rather let them go, flow through your development, achieve your outcomes, and swing back to help pull them towards their next levels.

We've all heard that your five closest friends are like gravity; you will involuntarily be pulled towards an overall average between the five of you in many areas. For example, you most likely earn a similar income to your five closest friends. Your physical condition is most likely in a similar place, your choice of conversation, foods, and activities are all most likely very similar. So again, the question remains, does this circle nurture and support your greatest dreams and goals? Or does it distract from them? You should surround yourself and spend your time and energy with those who have characteristics or core values, or a combination of both, you'd like to have as well.

If they nurture and support you, then that's amazing, and it's time to start sharing the knowledge of what you have learned during your developmental growth. You can all experience the amazing results together!

But, if your current circle is influencing you negatively, distracting you, or doesn't support your greatest dreams and goals, then it's time for change. It's time to evolve your team to the next level. Now, I'm not saying get rid of your long-time friendships. Sometimes it takes a lifetime to create those kinds of bonds of love and trust. What if you're trying to be an entrepreneur, a better father, a better and more loving significant other or get in shape? Your chances of being and doing those things greatly decreases if you surround yourself with lazy, complacent complainers. People who work at the same job they hate day in and day out and think you're crazy for wanting to retire early and better your life. Notice how I said, "YOU SURROUND YOURSELF WITH." It is a choice who you let share your time and energy. You have the freedom to make it. Are you building each other up or tearing each other down?

Let me share something super simple that you can do right now to help you identify your new mastermind group, AKA your "circle of influence." The RIGHT circle of influence. Your circle of positive influence. Refer to the "Circle of Influence" Worksheet by going to:

https://www.docdeliversbooks.com/free-ebook/

If you lack the sheet, simply get a piece of paper, and draw a vertical line down the center.

On the left side, fill in the people that support you, or even people who you would like to spend more time with. People who are likely to support you with positive reinforcement through the good or the bad. On the right side, make a list of those who pull you down, don't or won't support you, or are a negative influence. If you're honest with yourself, there will be some people that you have a hard time putting in the right column but there they are.

Do you have a lot of people in the left column? Or more in the right? Start to become aware of who you're spending time with and ask yourself if you have a solid circle of influence or not. From here comes the hard part. It's now time to make a commitment to yourself for the sake of your dreams and desired outcomes. It's time to minimize your exposure to those who are in the right column and begin adding new relationships to your left column, as well as nurturing the ones that are already there.

I promise you this. This will be one of the biggest causes of change in your life and one of the most powerful things you can ever do for yourself and your family. If you wish to vastly improve your life, this is a powerful way to do it! Breaking ties with people is hard, but if people in your life are draining you, it is time to let them go. A good friend should understand that you are seeking to better yourself.

Within your circle of influence, working with others who are working towards their own outcomes, you'll be able to inspire, motivate, and bounce ideas off one another, coming up with ideas you wouldn't have thought up on your own. You can choose to communicate weekly, bimonthly, or monthly depending on your varying schedules. One of the places that you can use to start the process of gaining people for your own Circle of Influence is by going to meetup.com.

Having a mentor to guide you during your continued journey

If you have formed your powerful mastermind group, establishing your Circle of Influence, I would still encourage you to look into getting a personal mentor as well. Your mastermind group can serve you well because there is strength in numbers, however there are potential limits on what you could accomplish. As I stated before, everyone within the circle is looking for support for their own outcomes so the attention may be divided, depending on the size of the group. However, one on one mentorship will provide that personalized touch, having someone's full and undivided attention on you can serve you well. When I think about mentors, I seek out those persons who have achieved success and their outcomes on a phenomenal level. People who have traveled a similar path to you, going through similar challenges and setbacks that you may encounter on your own.

Think of your mentor as your next level of accountability. With the right mentor, they keep you on track with your vision and help guide you more effectively towards your desired goals and outcomes.

When I first started on my journey of becoming an entrepreneur, I was fortunate enough to have a powerful Circle of Influence. I had success and made some moves forward; however, I was not achieving the level of outcomes that I felt I was capable of. I could see the bigger picture, however, as I began to "outgrow" my circle, I felt like I was stuck and couldn't make the pieces fit together. It was like I was staring at a giant jigsaw puzzle of my life and I didn't have all of the pieces.

The missing piece was not having a mentor to guide me and that was the element that made the picture clear and complete.

Yes, the circle served me and still does, however, the mentor that I would eventually select brought the game to a whole different level!

I felt, at first, that I didn't need a mentor because I didn't know what I didn't know.

When I finally got a mentor to personally guide me, I achieved more momentum in **two months** than I achieved in the previous *two years!*

My mentor helped me dig even deeper with my "why," having a deeper understanding of my path and the extra outcomes that would serve me well. Outcomes that I couldn't see or even conceive. That's because my mentor traveled the path that I was seeking, from full-time employee towards full-time entrepreneur. With my mentor, I transformed from small victories towards new levels of success. It was like high-level octane fuel was ignited within my soul, igniting my drive, thinking even bigger than I thought possible, and developing a deeper passion to achieve my outcomes no matter what.

Can you do it without a mentor?

Absolutely!

Think about this: If you had a mentor who could shave months, years perhaps, off your learning curve, would it be worth it to you? Once I decided to get a mentor, my only regret was not doing it sooner! I could have saved so much time, energy, finances, and frustration that the investment in my mentor would be miniscule compared to what I gained.

Trying to get to this level now without a mentor, becoming a successful author, entrepreneur, family man, athlete, speaker, and mentor myself would have been an unbelievable cost as far as time and resources.

Don't go at it alone.

Find the mentor who can serve you, guide you along your own outcomes, and help take you the next level of development. Let them help deliver an enhanced version of you.

CHAPTER 13
IN CLOSING...

November 18th, 2011.

The day that changed my life forever. The day I turned from being an employee to an unemployed and discarded cog in the corporate machine. In hindsight, it ended being one of the best days of my life because I realized I had two choices: Find the next job and begin the process of being comfortable and satisfied within my existing loop.

Or...

Start to develop the tools and resources that would unshackle me from my self-imposed pity party and live life on my own terms.

I had the freedom to choose my destiny and after making that choice, I will never look back. After many years of the highs and lows, victories, and defeats, I am not only proud of what I have accomplished but even more proud that I can share my journey of outcome achievements with you!

And now, I pass these tools to you, excited for your progress and the outcomes that you will achieve. I may not see your specific outcome, but as I visualize helping thousands of people as they read this book, I know that many lives are being reborn. People developing themselves as they transition from building the foundation of their lives, flowing through their developmental growth, and finally gaining the freedom to choose to grow and flow even further! And as the weeks and months progress, as you achieve your own outcomes, it will all be a reflection of the steps that you take today!

Remember this: You are a powerful person, capable of anything and everything that your desire.

Conceive your dreams, overcome your fears and challenges, and strive to deliver an enhanced version of you!

Your rebirth is waiting…

Go get it!!!

Chapter 14
Bonus Session

In order to give you the most value, I have complied all of the exercises and visualization scripts within one section on my author's page at https://www.docdeliversbooks.com/free-ebook/

Once you reach the site, simply scroll down to access all the worksheets and exercises. In addition, I have provided two bonus chapters to help you with the process. They are "Time Management" and "Morning and Evening Rituals." Go there to sign up for your bonus chapters as well!

Finally, there is an associated journal with this book titled, "Crushing Your Next 90 Daily Journal." Using it will help you organize, plan, and follow your actions towards your 90-day outcomes. It is available for sale through the link on the website at

https://www.docdeliversbooks.com/free-ebook/

If you wish to reach out to me and have me help you guide your own development and rebirth, you can email me at terence@terenceyoung.com. Let's chat and see how I can best serve you!

ACKNOWLEDGEMENTS

First, I would like to thank the higher powers for guiding me along this process. There were many times I wanted to rip the drafts up; however, my determination and persistence won the day.

Conceiving, writing, editing, and producing this book involved a ton of support so I would like to acknowledge and thank the following people:

John Hui, my personal mentor who helped guide me along the process and kept me on track. A fellow "Superhuman" who helped inspire me to bring out the best version of myself.

Kimberly Zink, Krystal Zellmer, Scott Pullan and Klemmer and Associates for introducing me to the world of personal development. My experiences with them as a student and coach have been invaluable.

Michael Bernoff, founder of the Human Communication Institute, for motivating and inspiring me to become more of what I thought I was capable of doing.

George Verongos, my super editor. Man, there were times I cursed your name, but in the end, I couldn't have done it without you! Thank you for believing in my message and helping to bring it out into a beautiful work!

My mom and dad, Barbara and Russell Young. You have always been there for me, picked me up when I fell, loved me when I didn't love myself and supported me along the paths I decided to walk. Thank you for everything you have given me! I love and appreciate my mother's inner calm and peace. I stand strong and tall with my father's discipline and tenacity. It's funny because my dad asked me several months ago, "Was I a good father?" I told him, "No, Dad. You were phenomenal, and I strive to be the father one day that you were to me!" I love you both!

To my sister Nioka. Watching you grow into the woman that you are warms my heart. Your determination to succeed, the balance you have forged as a wife and mother and having a powerful career in medicine makes me proud. You may be my little sister, but I admire and look up to you!

Last and definitely the most, my beautiful wife Yolanda. There were many long days and nights taken away from you while I was working on this. During these times, I know I could be a little unbearable and hard to deal with. Despite my cranky moods, you continued to inspire and support me along the way. Watching your personal transformation inspired me to write this book. Love you baby girl!

For all the friends and family who supported me, thank you! To my mighty tribe of "Superhumans" who are making the world better one person at a time, I admire your strength and courage, and it drives me to up my game even more! To acknowledge all of you would be a book within itself but you know who you are and that you are loved!

CPSIA information can be obtained
at www.ICGtesting.com
Printed in the USA
LVHW021704161218
600532LV00009B/85/P